SECRET
LONDON

A Guide to the City's Quirky & Unusual Sights

2nd Edition

Graeme Chesters

City Books • Bath • England

First published 2011 (as London's Hidden Secrets)
Reprinted (with changes) 2012
Reprinted (and updated) 2014
Reprinted (and updated) 2015
2nd Edition 2022

Copyright © 2011, 2012, 2014, 2015, 2022
Cover design: Derek Thompson
Cover photo © Paul Herbert (Adobe Stock)
Maps © Jim Watson

Survival Books Limited
Office 169, 3 Edgar Buildings, George Street, Bath BA1 2FJ, UK
+44 (0)1225-422884, info@survivalbooks.net
citybooks.co, survivalbooks.net, londons-secrets.com

British Library Cataloguing in Publication Data
A CIP record for this book is available
from the British Library.

ISBN: 978-1-913171-23-0

Printed via D'Print Pte Ltd.

Acknowledgements

The author would like to thank the many people who helped with research and provided information for this new second edition of *Secret London*. Special thanks are due to David Hampshire for updating and editing, Gwen Simmonds and Richard Todd for their invaluable research; Susan Griffith for additional editing; Grania Browning for final proof checking; John Marshall for desktop publishing and photo selection; Derek Thompson for cover design; Jim Watson for the maps; and the editor's wife for the constant supply of tea and coffee. Last, but not least, a special thank you to the many photographers – the unsung heroes – whose beautiful images bring the destinations to life.

Disabled Access

Many historic public and private buildings don't provide wheelchair access or provide wheelchair access to the ground floor only. Wheelchairs are provided at some venues (although users may need assistance) and you may also be able to hire a mobility 'scooter'. All museums, galleries and public buildings have a WC, although it may not be wheelchair accessible. Contact venues directly if you have specific requirements. The Accessable website (accessable.co.uk) provides in-depth access information for many destinations.

Readers' Guide

- **Address:** The entry's postcode and website (if applicable) are listed. You can enter the postcode to display a map of the location on Google and other map sites or, if you're driving, enter the postcode into your satnav.

- **Opening Hours: Note that opening times may vary from those listed due to the uncertainty wrought by the covid pandemic.** Many venues closed for an extended period during the pandemic and although most had re-opened at the time of going to press (March 2022), many were operating reduced opening hours. Some venues (such as museums and galleries) were also operating a pre-booking system via their websites. **It's therefore advisable to check directly with venues and confirm opening times and whether booking is required BEFORE visiting.** Many places are closed on bank holidays, particularly over the Christmas and New Year periods.

- **Cost:** Many museums and galleries provide free entry, including most major national collections and those run by local councils. National Trust and English Heritage sites are free to members (otherwise there's usually a hefty fee). Some cathedrals and churches levy an entrance fee, while others solicit donations (usually at least £5 per person) for their upkeep. Where applicable, fees are usually shown without the 'voluntary' gift aid donation added by many venues.

- **Transport:** The nearest tube or railway station is listed. Note that relatively few venues provide visitor parking, which may be impossible or prohibitively expensive in central London. It's advisable to travel by tube or rail, or – if this isn't possible – then by taxi.

Contents

10. Greater London – South 287

Index 315

Introduction

Writing (and updating) this book has been a pleasure, an education and a labour of love. This fully revised and updated second edition is long overdue – although frequently revised over the years – and delayed by the pandemic. Despite having lived in most areas of the city at various times, and happily pottered around it for many years, we now realise how much we had (and still have) to learn, and how many little-known delights London has to offer. Not only had we failed to visit many of the 139 'secret' places covered in this book, we hadn't even heard of many of them!

London is a city with a cornucopia of hidden treasures, being ancient, vast and in a constant state of flux. Newcomers have, of course, a wealth of world-renowned attractions to keep them occupied for a month of Sundays, which are more than adequately covered in a plethora of standard guide books. What *Secret London* does is take you off the beaten path to seek out the more unusual places that often fail to register on the radar of both visitors and residents alike. It aims to sidestep the chaos and queues of London's tourist-clogged attractions and visit its quirkier, more mysterious side.

Secret London includes some of the city's loveliest buildings, hidden gardens, bizarre museums, 'lost' graveyards, medieval pubs, cutting-edge art and design, and much more. The entries range from the enchanting canals of Little Venice to eccentric Thameside sculptures, from the stuffed remains of a philosopher to the poignant Foundling Museum, from the home of Sigmund Freud's famous sofa to where Handel and Hendrix meet, and from the spectacular treasures of Ham House to atmospheric Kensal Green cemetery.

Although *Secret London* isn't intended as a walking guide, many of the places covered are close to one another in central London – notably in the hubs of Westminster and the City – where you can easily stroll between them, while others are further out in the suburbs. However, all are close to public transport links and relatively easy to get to. And, conveniently for a city with a (largely unfounded) reputation for rain, many of the attractions are indoors, meaning you can visit them whatever the weather.

So there's no excuse for not getting out and exploring. I hope you enjoy discovering secret London as much as we did.

Graeme Chesters &
David Hampshire (editor)

March 2022

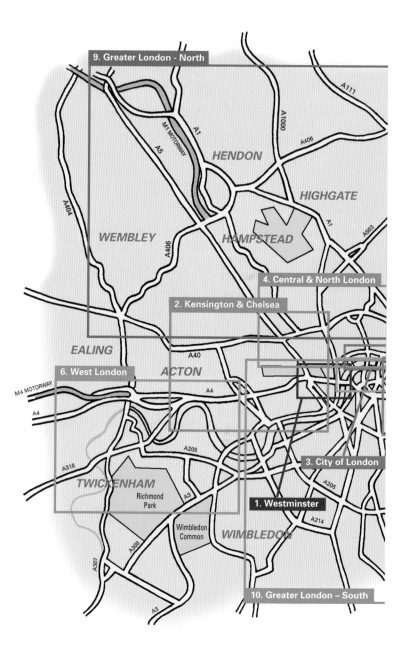

9. Greater London - North

4. Central & North London

2. Kensington & Chelsea

6. West London

3. City of London

1. Westminster

10. Greater London – South

HENDON

HIGHGATE

HAMPSTEAD

WEMBLEY

EALING

ACTON

TWICKENHAM

Richmond Park

Wimbledon Common

WIMBLEDON

M1 MOTORWAY

M4 MOTORWAY

A1

A5

A111

A1000

A406

A404

A406

A1

A503

A40

A4

A4

A205

A316

A3

A205

A214

A307

A308

A3

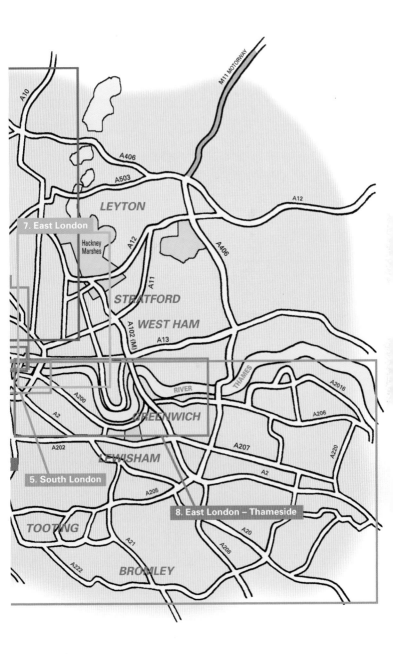

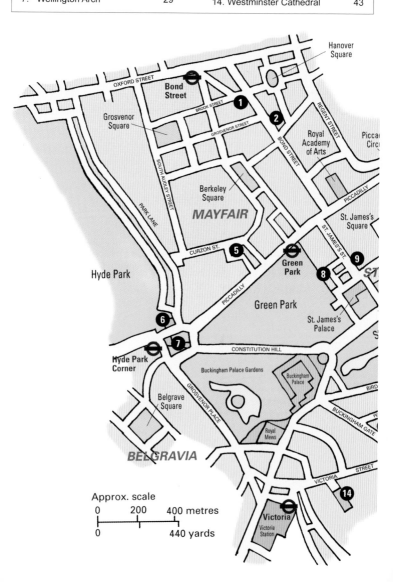

CHAPTER 1

WESTMINSTER

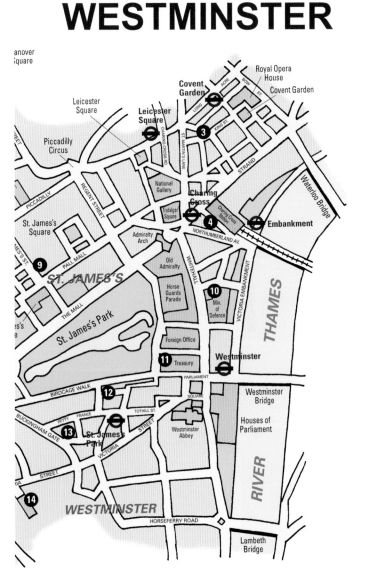

Address: 25 Brook St, W1K 4HB (020-7495 1685, handelhendrix.org).

Opening hours: Temporarily closed at the time of publication (summer 2022) while undergoing a major restoration. Check website for reopening.

Cost: See website.

Transport: Bond St tube.

George Frederic Handel

Jim Hendrix

HANDEL & HENDRIX IN LONDON

Handel & Hendrix in London comprises two residences: George Frederic Handel (1685-1759) house at 25 Brook Street and Jimi Hendrix's (1942-1970) flat on the top floor of 23 Brook Street. Handel's former home (Handel House) has been open to the public since November 2001, while Hendrix's flat was formerly the administrative office for staff. Number 25 is a restored Georgian building (Grade I listed) which was home to the noted baroque composer from 1723 until his death in 1759. It's where he composed some of his best works, including *Messiah*, *Zadok the Priest* and *Music for the Royal Fireworks*. The house celebrates the composer and his work with concerts, special events and exhibitions, all designed to bring Handel's world to life. Concerts are staged at the museum on a few days a week (see website for details).

The museum also aims to promote the musical and cultural heritage of 23 Brook Street, where rock legend Jimi Hendrix (1942-1970) rented a flat in 1968 with his then girlfriend, Kathy Etchingham; it's the musician's only surviving home. It's said that Hendrix was delighted to find himself living next door to Handel's old home and that he bought a lot of the composer's music. Some people even claim to hear Handel's influence in some of Hendrix's later compositions! Hendrix's bedroom has been restored to how it was in 1968-69 and contains a permanent exhibition that celebrates Hendrix's place in the musical and social world of '60s London, his influences and his legacy.

Handel House has finely-restored Georgian interiors and is dedicated to celebrating Handel and his work; frequent music rehearsals, concerts and special musical events in addition to regular displays and exhibitions bring Handel's world to life. There's also an impressive permanent display of Handel-related items, including the Handel House Collections acquired the Byrne Collection, a major Handel collection of several hundred objects, including books, letters, early editions of operas and oratorios, portraits, prints and sculpture. As can be seen from some of Handel's portraits, he was obviously a man with a healthy appetite. One of his early biographers, William Cox, put it succinctly, stating that he had 'a culpable indulgence in the sensual gratifications of the table'.

Handel was born in Halle, Germany, but became a British citizen in 1727. His Brook Street home was away from the artistic centres of Soho and Covent Garden but within easy walking distance of St James's Palace, where he conducted his official duties, and the King's Theatre, Haymarket, the focus of his Italian opera career at the time.

At the time of publication (summer 2022) the museum was closed and undergoing a major restoration and is planned to re-open in March 2023.

Henry Moore screen

Sekhmet effigy

Roosevelt and Churchill

BOND STREET SCULPTURES & STATUES

Bond Street doesn't actually exist! The only road connecting Piccadilly and Oxford Street is, in fact, two streets, Old Bond Street – built in the 1680s by Sir Thomas Bond – and New Bond Street, the stretch further north, which was created around 40 years later. It has recently become the most expensive retail location in Europe. However, as well as the glitz and glamour of the area's designer shopping outlets, it offers a number of works of art – sculptures and statues – that aren't always obvious unless you know where to look. The three described below are the most notable of a number on display. Keep your eyes peeled and keep looking up as you walk along the two Bond Streets.

At 34-35 New Bond Street, embedded above the entrance of the famous auction house Sotheby's, is London's oldest outdoor statue. It's an ancient Egyptian black basalt effigy of Sekhmet, the warrior goddess of Upper Egypt. Depicted as a lioness (the fiercest hunter known to the Egyptians), she was also a solar deity, bearing the solar disk and the uraeus (an upright form of spitting cobra). The statue dates from between 1600BC and 1320BC, and has been Sotheby's mascot since the 1880s when it was sold at auction for £40 but never collected by the buyer.

At 153 New Bond Street, look up to see four abstract pieces by Henry Moore which form a screen that adorns the Time and Life Building (the address is actually 1 Bruton Street). There's also a bronze by Moore inside, *Draped Reclining Figure*. The four external pieces are in a cubist style. Like Picasso (who Moore had met), Henry Moore was fascinated by African and Oceanic art, which can be seen in the angular, bulky figures depicted in this work. Moore carved them out of Portland stone in 1952 in his back garden and they were installed in 1953. He subsequently tried to buy them back, as he thought their position on the third floor was too high for them to be seen properly.

Where Old Bond Street becomes New Bond Street – near Asprey's, the jewellers – there's a high quality modern bronze (1995) entitled *Allies*, by the American sculptor Lawrence Holofcener. It shows Roosevelt and Churchill, sitting on a bench and chatting amiably, and was financed by the Bond Street Association to mark 50 years of peace. Churchill's mother was American and he and Roosevelt were actually distant cousins. After the war the two helped to found the United Nations.

Address: **WC2N 4LL.**

Opening hours: **Unrestricted access.**

Cost: **Free.**

Transport: **Leicester Sq or Covent Garden tube.**

GOODWIN'S COURT

This is another of London's time capsules. Walking along it is like stepping back into the 17th and 18th centuries (but thankfully without the filth, pestilence and religious persecution). It's a short, lovely alley, adjacent to 55-56 St Martin's Lane, and built into the front of the former Theatre Goers' Club of Great Britain. Goodwin's Court is easy to miss when travelling between Leicester Square and Covent Garden, and it's highly unlikely you'll stumble across it unless you're deliberately looking. The entrance from St Martin's Lane is simply a doorway off the street, with a couple of steps down, so keep a lookout for it.

On its south side is a row of narrow, attractive late 18th-century houses with bowed Georgian windows, which hint at the buildings' previous incarnation as a shops. There are polished black doors with shining knockers and doorknobs, with brass plates that announce the names of the businesses behind the doors.

It's more of an alley than a court – it isn't spacious enough to be the latter – and is an unusual survivor in an area that's seen much remodelling and redevelopment. Much of this was done by Inigo Jones on behalf of the Earl of Bedford. Among other things, they were responsible for the piazza in nearby Covent Garden.

Goodwin's Court is lit by three large, functioning gas lamps and at night the alley is atmospheric, magical even, in their flickering glow. It was previously known by the less attractive name of Fishers Alley, and although some people describe its atmosphere as Dickensian, it's much older than that. The current buildings first appear in local rate books in 1690, as a row of tailors. Although they don't have great architectural significance, they have an intimate charm and atmosphere. Not surprisingly, Goodwin's Court is popular as a film and television location.

It's just the type of place that comes to mind when thinking of Samuel Johnson's advice to his friend Boswell in the 18th century, on the occasion of the latter's arrival in London: 'survey its innumerable little lanes and courts'. Visitors today should keep an eye out for Goodwin's Court's fire marks, an interesting throwback to the time before a centralised fire brigade. In those days individual businesses had to insure against fire and an appropriate fire mark was displayed outside the building so that if a fire broke out, the fire fighting teams would know whether to tackle it or leave the building to burn. Goodwin's Court is lucky to still have them as they're apparently very collectable.

Address: 36 Craven St, WC2N 5NF (020-7839 2006, benjaminfranklinhouse.org).

Opening hours: Noon to 5pm, Friday to Sunday. The 'Historical Experience' show (ca. 1 hour) is available on Saturdays and Sundays at noon, 1pm, 2pm, 3.15pm and 4.15pm. Architectural tours (ca. 1 hour) are available on Fridays at 1pm. Groups are limited to a maximum of ten.

Cost: Historical experience: £8 adults, £6 seniors and students, under 16s free. Architectural tour: £6 adults, £4 seniors and students, under 16s free.

Transport: Charing Cross tube/rail or Embankment tube.

Benjamin Franklin

BENJAMIN FRANKLIN HOUSE

While sympathetic to the view that visiting a museum dedicated to a man known for discoveries about electricity and for being a politician might be less than thrilling, we urge you to try this intriguing, well-conceived exhibit. The Grade I listed, architecturally-important house was built around 1730 and retains many original features, including the central staircase, lathing, panelling, stoves, windows, beams and more.

It's the world's only remaining home of Benjamin Franklin, which opened on 17th January 2006 on the anniversary of his 300th birthday. Franklin (1706-1790) was born in Boston, Massachusetts to an American mother and a British father. He lived and worked in this house for 16 years, on the eve of the American Revolution, and it has a special place in Anglo-American history, being the first de facto US embassy.

Benjamin Franklin's work as a philosopher, printer and more contributed to the Age of Enlightenment, and his scientific work meant that he came to be regarded as the father of electricity. As if this wasn't enough for one person, he was also a key founder of the United States, the only statesman to sign all four documents that created the new nation.

This is an inventive museum, which offers a good flavour of Franklin's many achievements and of the times in which he lived. The 'Student Science Centre' allows the recreation of experiments from his time in London, while the 'Scholarship Centre' on the top floor is a centre for the study of the many subjects that Franklin was involved with.

The Historical Experience takes a 'museum as theatre' approach, an innovative, entertaining way of presenting history. You're 'accompanied' by an actress who plays Polly Hewson, Franklin's landlady's daughter, who became like a daughter to him. The live performance, along with lighting, sound and visual projections, brings the whole 18th-century experience to life.

To end on a grisly note, the remains of four adults and six children were found at the property when it was being restored. Franklin's landlady's daughter Polly married a surgeon, who ran an anatomy school here. There's a small exhibit in the basement about medical history, which displays some of the 'Craven Street bones'.

SHEPHERD MARKET

This hidden enclave, only a stone's throw from Green Park and elegant St James's, is described on the website as 'London's best-kept secret'. It's a tiny series of closely packed streets tucked away between Piccadilly and Curzon Street in the exclusive district of Mayfair. The term Mayfair comes from the fair that used to take place on the site where Shepherd Market now sits. It was banned in 1708 because it had become boisterous and attracted troublemakers, and it was decided that building on the site was the best way to prevent their return.

Shepherd Market was developed in 1735-1746 by Edward Shepherd, a local architect and developer, who was active in many parts of Mayfair. It was built to house shopkeepers and other traders to serve the large houses of Piccadilly, and the Market would have thronged with their servants buying goods and services. Part of its attraction is that it has managed to retain its modest 18th-century feel, and is a reminder of the Georgians' facility with attractive, useful town planning.

During the '20s, Shepherd Market was a highly fashionable address. Next to it is Half Moon Street, where the fictional upper class twit Bertie Wooster and his wise valet Jeeves lived (characters created by the English writer P. G. Wodehouse). Nowadays Shepherd Market is known for its intimate restaurants, boutiques and Victorian pubs – a pedestrianised escape from central London's hustle and bustle, but only a five-minute stroll from Green Park tube.

Many of the old market shops are now outdoor cafés and restaurants, but there's also a range of interesting specialist shops, many selling artwork, jewellery and antiques. The crowds in the Market's Victorian pubs often spill onto the streets, weather permitting, which adds to the atmosphere. Shepherd Market is best approached from Curzon Street via a covered passageway at number 47, which leads into the Market's network of alleys and streets.

The area used to be regarded as Mayfair's red light district, but although such trade has now largely moved elsewhere, the old reputation for vice was rekindled in the '80s when Shepherd Market was the venue for trysts between the highly successful novelist and Conservative party deputy chairman Jeffrey Archer and prostitute Monica Coghlan. Reports about this appeared in the *Daily Star*, but Archer denied it and won damages from the paper. Later, he was judged to have lied in court about the matter, was jailed and had to repay the damages he'd been awarded against the *Star*.

AT A GLANCE

Address: 149 Piccadilly, Hyde Park Cnr, W1J 7NT (020-7499 5676, english-heritage.org.uk/visit/places/apsley-house).

Opening hours: See website for opening times.

Cost: See website for information. English Heritage members free.

Transport: Hyde Park Corner tube.

Duke of Wellington

APSLEY HOUSE

This Grade I listed building and residence of the Dukes of Wellington stands alone at Hyde Park Corner, on the southeast corner of Hyde Park. It's run by English Heritage as a museum and art gallery, although the current Duke of Wellington still uses part of the building as his London home.

Apsley House is sometimes known as Number One, London, as it was the first house seen by visitors after passing through the toll gates at Knightsbridge. Another nickname is the Wellington Museum. The house was originally built in red brick by Robert Adam (an influential Scottish neoclassical architect) between 1771 and 1778 for Lord Apsley, the Lord Chancellor. Some of Adam's interiors survive. It was acquired by the Duke of Wellington in 1817, who faced the house's brick walls with Bath stone, added the Corinthian portico and enlarged the property.

The interior has changed little since it was the home of the Iron Duke in the years following his victory over Napoleon at Waterloo. Many of the rooms were redesigned to reflect his growing status and influence (he was also a politician, becoming Prime Minister in 1828), and were a perfect setting for entertaining, including hosting an annual Waterloo Banquet to commemorate the famous victory, which continues to this day.

The 7th Duke gave the house and most of its contents to the nation in 1947, but the Duke retains the right to occupy just over half the property. The family's apartments are on the north side of the house, mainly on the second floor. The rest of the building is open to the public – the dazzling interiors are a magnificent example of Regency style – and there's a splendid collection of paintings and artworks that's one of the most intriguing in London and not nearly as well known as it should be.

There are over 200 paintings (some of them part of the Spanish Royal collection, which came into the Duke's possession after the Battle of Vitoria in 1813 – they'd been plundered from Spanish royal palaces by Napoleon Bonaparte's brother Joseph), including works by Brueghel the Elder, Goya, Landseer, Murillo, Rubens, Van Dyck and Velasquez.

On show are also the many gifts that the first Duke received from European rulers in gratitude for his military successes, including candelabras, porcelain, silver and gilt items, trophies, uniforms and weapons. A colossal (3.45m-high) nude marble statue of Napoleon by Canova stands in pride of place on the stairwell in the middle of the house.

Address: Apsley Way, Hyde Park Corner, W1J 7JZ (020-7930 2726, english-heritage.org.uk/visit/places/wellington-arch).

Opening hours: Wed-Sun, 10am to 5pm. Closed 24-27th Dec, 31st Dec and 1st Jan.

Cost: £6 adults, £5.30 concessions, £3.60 children (5-17), £15.60 families (2 adults and up to 3 children). English Heritage members free.

Transport: Hyde Park Corner tube.

WELLINGTON ARCH

This triumphal arch lies to the south of Hyde Park and at the northwest corner of Green Park, and sits on a traffic island, so is sometimes ignored. This is a pity as it has an interesting history and the views from the top alone justify the price of admission.

It's sometimes called Constitution Arch or the Green Park Arch and was built in 1826-30. Designed by Decimus Burton, much of the intended exterior decoration was omitted in order to save money after the King had overspent on the refurbishment of Buckingham Palace, which was going on at the same time. The Arch was built both to commemorate victory over Napoleon and as an outer gateway to Constitution Hill and hence as a grand entrance into central London from the west.

It originally stood opposite Apsley House (see page 27), which was known as Number One London, as it was the first property visitors from the countryside encountered after passing through the toll gates at Knightsbridge, but the Arch was moved a short distance (around 100 yards) in 1882-3 to allow for a road-widening scheme.

It was originally crowned with a massive statue of the Duke of Wellington (8.5m high and weighing 40 tons), the largest equestrian figure ever made, but it was so large that it attracted ridicule, making the Arch look like a footstool. It remained there during the Duke of Wellington's lifetime (it was thought by many, including Queen Victoria, that the old duke, who lived so close – in Apsley House – might be insulted if it was removed) and was moved to Aldershot in 1883 at the same time as the Arch itself was moved. It was eventually replaced (in 1912) by a large bronze quadriga (a chariot drawn by four horses), depicting the angel of peace descending on the chariot of war, which is Europe's largest bronze sculpture.

The Arch itself is hollow, and used to house London's second-smallest police station (the smallest is in Trafalgar Square). It's now owned by English Heritage and has three floors of exhibits detailing its varied history. There are terraces on both sides at the top, commanding excellent views of Hyde Park Corner, Hyde Park, the junction of Park Lane and Piccadilly, Green Park, Constitution Hill and even parts of Buckingham Palace's private gardens. The views alone are reason enough to visit the Arch, but if you don't want to put your hand in your pocket take a stroll past it after dark, when creative floodlighting dramatises the sculpture.

Address: 27 St James's Pl, SW1A 1NR (020-7514 1958, spencerhouse.co.uk, email: tours@spencerhouse.co.uk).

Opening hours: Sun (except August) 10am to 4.30pm. Access is by guided tour (ca. 1hr) only (maximum 20). Timed tickets are on sale from 10am on the day or can be booked in advance via the website (spencerhouse.co.uk/book-your-tour). Groups of 15-60 people can also visit on Monday mornings.

Cost: £15 adults, £12 concessions (students, seniors and under-16s). Children must be accompanied by an adult.

Transport: Green Park tube.

SPENCER HOUSE

According to its website, this is 'London's most magnificent private palace'. It's certainly one of the capital's best examples of a Palladian mansion, conceived as a showcase of classical design and a visual treat for the visitor. Spencer House was built in 1756-66 for the Spencer family by the Palladian architect John Vardy, who was replaced in 1758 by James 'Athenian' Stuart, who did the interiors (the façades are Vardy's). The house thus became the first in London with accurate Greek interior detailing and one of the first (and finest) examples of the neo-classical style that was to sweep the country.

The house was conceived as a showcase of classical design but was also designed for pleasure, and a festive theme runs through the decoration of the many state rooms that were used for receptions and family gatherings. The first Earl Spencer (an ancestor of Diana, Princess of Wales) and his wife were prominent figures in London society, and the house often hosted lavish entertainments. Their descendants, notably the fourth and sixth Earls, both of whom served as Lord Chamberlain of the Royal Household, continued this tradition.

Spencer House is one of the last remaining of the many private palaces that once adorned central London. It's a great showcase of sophisticated, 18th-century aristocratic taste, lavishly furnished with elaborate period paintings (including some by Reynolds), objets d'art and furniture. A number of beautifully restored state rooms are open to the public.

There are magnificent views over Green Park and a spectacular garden, although it's only open to the public on a few days a year in spring or summer (see the website for details). The garden was designed by Henry Holland (the architect employed by the second Earl Spencer in the 1790s), possibly in collaboration with Lavinia, Countess Spencer; when it was planted in July 1798 it was one of the largest gardens in Piccadilly. It has recently been replanted with plants and shrubs appropriate to the late 18th and 19th centuries.

The Spencer family lived in the house until 1926, since when it has been let it to a variety of tenants. It's currently leased by Lord (4th Baron) Rothschild for one of his companies, and he's extensively (and expensively) restored the building at a cost of many millions of pounds. Much of the work was done in the late '80s and it's thought by many to be one of the best examples of a building restoration and London's finest surviving 18th-century townhouse.

Address: **3 St James's St, SW1A 1EG (0800-280 2440, bbr.com).**

Opening hours: **No longer a retail outlet (now at 63 Pall Mall, SW1Y 5HZ, Tue-Fri, 10am to 7pm; Sat 10am to 6pm; closed Sundays and bank holidays). The St James's HQ hosts a range of events and tastings (see website for information) and cellars that can be hired for receptions and private dining.**

Cost: **Free.**

Transport: **Green Park tube.**

Pickering Place

BERRY BROTHERS & RUDD & PICKERING PLACE

The BBR cellar resembles a historical time capsule. It's the HQ of Britain's oldest wine and spirit merchant, which has traded from the same premises for over 300 years. The business was officially established in 1698 by a certain Widow Bourne, and the company evolved from selling coffee, tea, spices and other provisions to fine wines and whisky.

The premises are redolent of a bygone age and has changed little over its long years in business, the floors and wood-panelled walls being agreeably crooked. On show inside are important artefacts and documents from the company's distinguished history. Berry Brothers and Rudd first supplied wine to the Royal Family during the reign of George III and continues to do so today, with two current royal warrants for HM The Queen and HRH the Prince of Wales. The staff are friendly and approachable, and you can treat yourself to wines costing from £10 to £10,000 per bottle. You'll be in esteemed company: customers have included Lord Byron, William Pitt and the Aga Khan, to name drop just a few.

This modestly sized 'shop' is renowned for being able to supply huge quantities of wine almost at the drop of a hat. The reason is beneath your feet. Its vast cellars (previously part of Henry VIII's residence) contain around 200,000 bottles and run under the courtyard outside as far as Pall Mall. Parts of the cellars can be hired for receptions and private dining (Berry Brothers has its own catering team) – see bbr.com/events-experiences/our-spaces.

Next door to Berry Brothers is Pickering Place, Britain's smallest public square. It's a Georgian delight and resembles a charming outdoor room. Berry Brothers owns one of its lovely William and Mary-era townhouses, which is available for private hire. Pickering Place has a varied history, being situated on a site that was part of a medieval maidens' leper colony and later the location of Henry VIII's tennis court. Part of this structure can be seen when walking down the short passage (timbered and dating to 1730) from St James's Street.

The present square dates from 1734. Duels with swords used to be fought here, inside its enclosed, discreet perimeter. There was also the odd pistol duel, and it's claimed to be the site of the last public duel in England, although there are other claims for this 'honour'. Pickering Place is still lit by its original gaslights and is particularly atmospheric at dusk when they are lit.

BANQUETING HOUSE

This is one of the hidden delights of Westminster, often overlooked by the many visitors who throng the streets around Whitehall. It's the only remaining part of the Palace of Whitehall, which was the main residence of English monarchs in London from 1530 until 1698, when all except Inigo Jones's 1622 Banqueting House was destroyed by fire. Before the fire, the palace had grown to become the largest in Europe, larger even than the Vatican and Versailles.

The Banqueting House is significant in the history of English architecture, being the first building to be built in the neo-classical style that would sweep the country. It was designed by Jones in a style influenced by Palladio, an Italian Renaissance architect, himself influenced by Greek and Roman architecture. Inigo Jones was a revolutionary architect and designer whose work shook up English building design in the early 17th century.

The Banqueting House was controversially refaced with Portland stone in the 19th century, although the details of the original façade were carefully preserved. Today, the building is Grade I listed and cared for by the independent charity, Historic Royal Palaces. It's spread over three floors and the term 'Banqueting House' is something of a misnomer, as it's a hall that was used not just for banquets but also for ceremonies, royal receptions and the performance of masques (a cross between a ball, an amateur dramatic production, a play and a fancy dress party, which was an entertainment as well as a way of expressing ideas about royal authority, responsibility and privileges).

The building's major attraction is its richly-painted ceiling (opposite), a masterpiece by the Antwerp-based artist and diplomat Peter Paul Rubens, the only surviving in-situ ceiling painted by him. It was commissioned by Charles I and celebrates the benefits of wise rule and his father's flawed idea of the Divine Right of Kings. Therefore it's rather ironic that Charles I, as a result of his unwise rule, was beheaded on a scaffold erected outside the hall in 1649, after losing the Civil War (1642-49). It's fortunate that the ceiling survived the short period of Puritan rule that followed: Cromwell took over the building as his hall of audience in 1654, but he died in 1658 and the monarchy was restored in 1660.

Address: Clive Steps, King Charles St, SW1A 2AQ (020-7930 6961, iwm. org.uk/visits/churchill-war-rooms).

Opening hours: Daily, 9.30am to 6pm (closed 24-26th December).

Cost: £26.35 adults, £23.60 concessions, £13.15 children (5-15), under 5s free.

Transport: Westminster or St James's Park tube.

Sir Winston Churchill

CHURCHILL WAR ROOMS

This is one of five branches of the Imperial War Museum, comprising the Cabinet War rooms, an underground complex that housed a British government command centre during the Second World War, and the Churchill Museum, which is devoted to the life of Sir Winston Churchill.

The construction of the Cabinet War Rooms began in 1938 and became operational in August 1939, shortly before the outbreak of war. They were the nerve centre of Britain's war effort, equipped with accommodation, offices, communications and broadcasting equipment, sound-proofing, ventilation and reinforcement. During the Blitz it was decided to increase the protection of the War Rooms by installing a massive layer of concrete up to 5ft thick, known as 'the Slab'.

Around 30 of the historic rooms can be viewed, including the typing pool, the dormitories and Churchill's bedroom, which along with the museum are evocative of the period. The Map Room and Cabinet Room were of particular importance, the former manned around the clock by officers of the Royal Navy and producing a daily intelligence report for the Prime Minister, the military Chiefs of Staff and the King.

Two other notable rooms include the Transatlantic Telephone Room and Churchill's office-bedroom. From 1943, the former housed an encrypted telephone enabling Churchill to speak securely with President Roosevelt in Washington. Churchill's office-bedroom contained BBC broadcasting equipment and he made a number of wartime broadcasts from here. Although the office room was fitted out as a bedroom, Churchill rarely slept underground, preferring to sleep at 10 Downing Street or at the No.10 Annexe (directly above the Cabinet War Rooms).

The rooms are almost exactly as they were when they were last used in 1945, with the walls still plastered with maps covered in pins showing troop movements. In the Cabinet Room, 115 cabinet meetings were held, sometimes until after midnight (Churchill was noted for retiring late). The rooms on display are only a small part of a much larger complex, extending over a number of acres.

The Churchill Museum is cutting edge, innovative and interactive, using technology and multimedia to cover all aspects of Churchill's long and varied life (1874-1965), private and public, triumphs and failures. It's advisable to allow a minimum of 90 minutes for a visit to the site, but in view of the number of rooms to explore, the amount of information to digest, and the attractions of the on-site café, many visitors stay for half a day or more (which may account for the high entrance fee).

Queen Anne

QUEEN ANNE'S GATE

Queen Anne's Gate boasts some of the city's best Queen Anne architecture, but is often overlooked by those heading to nearby St James's' Park and the Queen Elizabeth II Conference Centre. It's well worth seeking out, however, as the street has a range of fine pink and white houses, with splendidly ornate porches, delicate iron railings and interesting touches, such as the cone-shaped torch snuffer outside number 26. Several of the houses have elaborate wooden canopies.

Queen Anne (1665-1714) ascended the thrones of England, Scotland and Ireland in 1702, and in 1707 England and Scotland were united as a single sovereign state, the Kingdom of Great Britain. Anne hence became Great Britain's first sovereign, while continuing to hold the separate crown as Queen of Ireland and the title of Queen of France.

In Britain, the Queen Anne style means either the English Baroque architectural style, popular around the time of Queen Anne's reign (1702-14), or a revived form which was popular in the late 19th and early 20th centuries. (In other countries, it means rather different things, notably in the US and Australia.)

Queen Anne's Gate was originally two closes separated by a wall where a statue of Queen Anne now stands (see below). The wall was removed in the 1870s and the western close became Queen Square and the eastern one Park Street. Most of the houses in the former Park Street are late 18th-century. Numbers 6-12 date from the 1830s. Lord Palmerston (a British statesman who twice served as Prime Minister in the mid-19th century) was born at number 20 in 1784, while jurist, philosopher and social reformer Jeremy Bentham owned number 40, and let it to his friend the historian, economist and political theorist James Mill and his son, the influential philosopher John Stuart Mill. The houses in the former Queen Square are older, most dating from 1704 when the street was built.

With the notable exception of Queen Victoria (who has dozens), there's a lack of statues of women in London, but Queen Anne has a respectable two. The one at Queen Anne's Gate is a copy of one at St Paul's Cathedral (she was the ruling monarch when St Paul's was completed – it was declared officially complete by Parliament on Christmas Day 1711). Her ghost is said to walk three times around Queen Anne's Gate on the anniversary of her death, July 31st, which surely makes this the ideal date to visit.

AT A GLANCE

Address: 23 Caxton St, SW1H 0PY (en.wikipedia.org/wiki/blewcoat_school).

Opening hours: Unrestricted access to the exterior (which is the main attraction). The building is currently an exclusive boutique.

Cost: Free.

Transport: St James's Park tube.

Statue above door

BLEWCOAT SCHOOL

This is a gem of a building, an elegant early 18th-century detached townhouse of red brick sitting unexpectedly among undistinguished modern office blocks. It isn't known who the architect was, but it's built in Sir Christopher Wren's style, so even if he had no direct involvement he seems to have been influential.

It was built in 1709 as a school for poor children. The man behind it (and who paid for the building) was William Green, a local brewer and owner of the Stag brewery. He wanted a charity school to teach pupils how to 'read, write, cast accounts and the catechism'. The school itself was founded in 1688, and its first building was in Duck Lane, established for the education of 'fifty poor boys likely to thrive by scholarship'.

The founder stated that the boys must come from the parish of St Mary's (the church next door to Westminster Abbey). Girls were later schooled here – 20 were admitted in 1713, which was very unusual for the time – but this stopped around 1876, although the reason is unclear.

The building was a school until the '20s or '30s (there's some confusion about the exact date), and during the Second World War was used as an army store. The National Trust purchased it in 1954, and used it as a gift shop and information centre until 2012 (which seems rather prosaic for such an architectural gem).

The Blewcoat is small, symmetrical and somewhat Dutch-looking, seemingly rather out of place, adrift even, among the faceless surrounding buildings, and its attractiveness is at variance with the fact that it dates from a time when this part of London was one of its largest slums – then, as now, it must have stood out. It has a beautifully proportioned interior, around 42ft long and 30ft wide, with its floor raised several feet above the surrounding road and ground surfaces.

At the entrance from Caxton Street is a Corinthian-columned vestibule carrying the original external clock chamber. A life-sized painted wooden carving of a Blewcoat charity boy, wearing his blue coat, still stands above the doorway, a reminder of how the school provided an education for poor children. Very pleasing on the eye, the building has an air of solidity and tranquillity about it.

Address: 42 Francis St, SW1P 1QW (020-7798 9055, westminstercathedral.org.uk).

Opening hours: Daily 7am to 9pm, except Saturdays, 8am to 7pm. Tower viewing gallery and museum, 9.30am to 5pm (6pm Sat-Sun).

Cost: Entry to the cathedral is free, but lift access to the tower viewing gallery is £6 for adults, £3 concessions. The Treasures of Westminster Cathedral (museum) is £5 for adults, £2.50 concessions, £11 families (two adults and up to four children).

Transport: Victoria tube/rail.

WESTMINSTER CATHEDRAL

Not to be confused with the famous Westminster Abbey (the mother church of the Church of England), which invariably overshadows it, Westminster Cathedral is the largest Catholic church in England and Wales, and the mother church of the English and Welsh Catholic community. Unlike the Abbey, it's a relatively modern building; construction began in 1895 and it opened in 1903. It wasn't consecrated until 1910, owing to church laws at the time that nowhere could be consecrated until it was free from debt and all of its fabric was completed.

Westminster Cathedral isn't a conventional late-Victorian building, but was modelled on a Byzantine basilica, made of brick, with the interior decorated with marble and mosaics. The outside resembles a wedding cake, with pseudo-Byzantine copper domes and a terracotta bell tower with white Portland stone stripes. However, it's little visited, except by Catholics, the surrounding Victorian mansion blocks seeming to hide it, even in this busy part of London.

The bell tower rises elegantly to 273 feet with a viewing gallery 210 feet above street level commanding spectacular views. The interior of the cathedral contains fine marble work and mosaics, while the 14 Stations of the Cross by sculptor Eric Gill are majestic. Some 126 different varieties of marble decorate the cathedral, probably more than in any other building in England. They come from 24 countries on five continents, including many that were used in ancient Greece and Rome. The mosaics are exotic, with gold and shades of blue.

Gill's 14 panels (each 5ft 8in square) were carved in low relief in Hopton Wood limestone. The sculptor was unknown at the time (he produced the design in 1914) and anxious for a large commission, therefore he charged a very low fee. He'd become a Catholic just six months earlier, which was one of the reasons he got the job. Reactions to the panels were mixed: some found them cold, pagan even, while others admired their breadth and simplicity of design.

As a final bonus, the cathedral has a splendid choir – one of the country's best – that sings mass most evenings, providing an atmospheric, free concert.

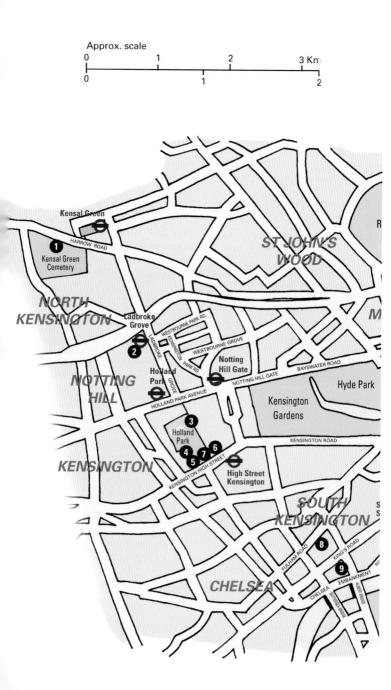

CHAPTER 2

KENSINGTON & CHELSEA

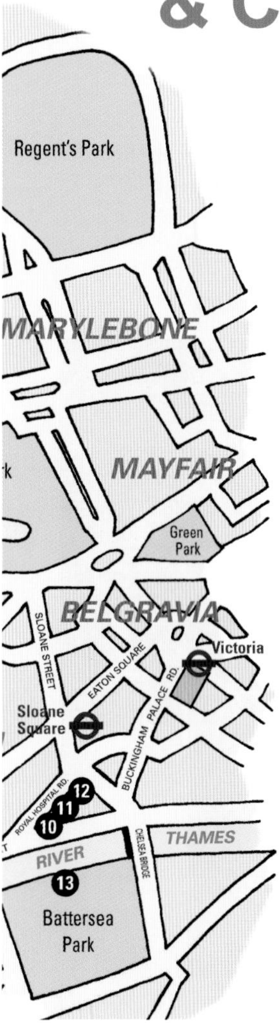

Regent's Park

MARYLEBONE

MAYFAIR

Green Park

BELGRAVIA

SLOANE STREET

EATON SQUARE

BUCKINGHAM PALACE RD

Victoria

Sloane Square

ROYAL HOSPITAL RD

12

11

10

KINGS ROAD

THAMES

RIVER

13

Battersea Park

Address: Harrow Rd, W10 4RA (020-8969 0152, kensalgreencemetery. com and kensalgreen.co.uk/tours.php).

Opening hours: Apr-Sep: Mon-Sat, 9am to 6pm, Sun 10am to 6pm. Oct-Mar: Mon-Sat, 9am to 5pm, Sun 10am to 5pm. Bank holidays, including Christmas Day, 10am to 1.30pm.

Cost: Free to wander around on your own; guided tours (2 hours) £12 'donation', Sundays 2pm from Mar-Oct and the first and third Sunday of the month Nov-Feb.

Transport: Kensal Green tube/rail.

KENSAL GREEN CEMETERY

Kensal Green is an undistinguished, slightly shabby part of northwest London, but it plays host to one of the capital's most beautiful (if ramshackle) cemeteries. The access point to the cemetery is unpromising, from the traffic-choked Harrow Road, with its plethora of fast-food joints and second-hand shops. But enter and it's like being in the countryside, full of mature shrubs and trees, which help make the cemetery one of London's richest and most important wildlife habitats.

Kensal Green opened in 1833, making it London's oldest public burial ground. It's one of the so-called 'Magnificent Seven', the other six being Abney Park (see page 285), Brompton, Highgate, Nunhead (see page 297), Tower Hamlets and West Norwood. It's the largest and most opulent of these Victorian cemeteries, containing around 250,000 bodies. It has a heady mix of architectural styles, with graves from the 1700s to the 1990s, often sited close together with little apparent order or pattern to its layout. There are a number of Grade I and II listed buildings and tombs, and the whole cemetery is Grade II listed. It's an interesting blend of Georgian splendour, Victorian decadence, 19th-century Gothic and modern styles.

There are two ways to visit: on a two-hour guided tour (see box opposite) or by exploring it yourself. Wear stout shoes or boots, as the terrain is uneven and often muddy. Vast tracts of the cemetery are nature and wildlife reserves, hence their overgrown state. The eastern end of the cemetery has a butterfly and bee garden, home to plants designed to attract them such as bergamot, hyssop, rosemary and sage. The cemetery is a place where it pays just to wander, while getting slightly lost and stumbling across a plethora of visual and architectural treats.

Near the cemetery's chapel are Georgian catacombs in the form of a colonnade, crumbling but atmospheric and well worth visiting. Kensal Green has a number of famous 'residents' you might wish to seek out, including the Brunel family of engineers, in a surprisingly understated tomb in a quiet corner of the cemetery. It's also the last resting place of the children of George III, authors Wilkie Collins and Anthony Trollope, and playwright Terence Rattigan.

Address: **111-117 Lancaster Rd, W11 1QT (020-7243 9611, museumofbrands.com).**

Opening hours: **Mon-Sat, 10am to 6pm; Sun and bank holidays, 11am to 5pm.**

Cost: **£9 (including gift aid) adults, £7 concessions (incl. students), £5 children (7-16), £24 families.**

Transport: **Ladbroke Grove tube.**

Robert Opie

MUSEUM OF BRANDS

This is one of London's smaller, specialised museums that at first sight might appear dull or too obscure, but is actually fascinating. A recent addition to the roster of London museums (from 1984 to 2001, the collection was housed in a museum in Gloucester, moving to London in 2005), it's situated near buzzy, visitor-choked Portobello Market. It moved to its current location in 2015 after outgrowing its previous site, adding new galleries, event spaces and a garden.

The Museum of Brands is the work of Robert Opie, an author and consumer historian who was eager to record the history of the products around us. He started his collection at the age of 16 (with a packet of Munchies) and it has expanded to encompass all aspects of daily life: design, fashion, magazines, souvenirs, technology, toys, travel and much more. As well as the permanent collection, there are special exhibitions (see website for details).

The permanent display features over 12,000 items from the Robert Opie Collection and explores the history of consumer culture over the past 200 years through household products, from Victorian times to the present day. The collection shows how famous brands have evolved through their creative use of packaging and advertising. Appropriately, the museum is sponsored by many leading brands, including Cadbury, Diageo, Kellogg's, McVitie's, Piglobal, Twinings and Vodafone.

It's a well-organised and engaging museum, which will evoke waves of nostalgia in anybody born before around 1990. This is especially the case when watching some of the old television commercials, which are notably evocative of their period and of how our lives were at the time. The collection gives a great insight into changing trends, designs and fashions, as well as providing a social history of British consumer society.

Anybody connected with the creative industries – advertising, art, branding, design, fashion, graphic design, packaging et al – will find this museum educational and inspirational, and you can take some of that home with you as the shop sells merchandise related to the collection.

AT A GLANCE

Address: Ilchester Pl, W8 6LU (rbkc.gov.uk/leisure-and-culture/parks/holland-park).

Opening hours: Daily, 7.30am until 30 minutes before dusk.

Cost: Free.

Transport: Holland Park or High Street Kensington tube.

Dutch Garden

Holland House (now a youth hostel)

HOLLAND PARK & KYOTO GARDEN

Holland Park (the area) is an affluent, fashionable part of west London, dotted with large Victorian townhouses and upmarket restaurants and shops. It's one of the capital's most expensive residential districts and therefore an appropriate location for arguably London's most peaceful and romantic park. Yet it's a park that's either unknown or ignored by many who aren't local residents.

At a mere 54 acres (22ha), Holland Park is one of the capital's smAt a mere 54 acres (22.5ha), Holland Park is one of the capital's smallest public parks, but has plenty to offer: beautiful views, gardens, sports areas, peacocks, an ecology centre, some of the city's best children's play facilities, a café, large areas of woodland and a Japanese (Kyoto) garden. The park is also a renowned picnic spot, with plenty of secluded hideaways in a variety of environments.

Holland Park was formerly the grounds of Cope Castle, a large Jacobean mansion dating from the early 17th century, built for Sir Walter Cope, James I's Chancellor. It was one of the area's first great houses, later renamed Holland House, but it was almost destroyed during a ten-hour bombing raid in 1940; one wing remains, part of which is the London Holland Park youth hostel (see hostelworld.com/hosteldetails.php/safestay-london-kensington-holland-park), possibly the capital's most attractive. In the summer, opera performances are staged by Opera Holland Park (operahollandpark.com) under a temporary canopy, with the remains of Holland House as a backdrop.

The park is roughly divided into three areas: the northern half is semi-wild woodland, in which the sounds of the city all but disappear; the central part – around the remains of Holland House – is more formal, with a number of formal garden areas; while the southern part is used for sport.

The highlight of Holland Park for many people is beautiful Kyoto Garden, a Japanese garden donated by the Chamber of Commerce in Kyoto in 1991 to celebrate the Japan Festival which was held in London in 1992. Refurbished in 2001, the garden is immaculately kept and widely regarded as one of London's most tranquil places. It has a lovely pond, with stepping stones, and a 15ft waterfall. It's surrounded by elegant plantings of Japanese shrubs and trees, which are at their best in spring and autumn, offering an ever-changing variety of vivid colours.

Address: 29 Melbury Rd, W14 8AB (en.wikipedia.org/wiki/the_tower_house).

Opening hours: The interior of the house isn't open to the public, but the exterior has unrestricted access from the street.

Cost: Free.

Transport: High Street Kensington tube.

TOWER HOUSE

This striking, Grade I listed, late Victorian townhouse was designated number 9 Melbury Road until 1967, when it became number 29. It was built between 1876 and 1878 in 13th-century French Gothic style by the Victorian art-architect William Burges (1827-1881), as his home. Burges was the greatest of the Victorian art-architects and he sought in his work an escape from the pragmatism and industrialisation of the 19th century, and a return to the architectural and social values of (an imagined) medieval England.

This approach was appropriate for the part of London in which he chose to build, Holland Park, an area of Kensington which by the 1870s had become a Bohemian neighbourhood. It attracted artists and architects, notably Lord Leighton, the artist, whose Leighton House (see page 55) begun in 1866 was similar to Burges' property.

Burges used ideas from his other work in elements of the interior and exterior design of Tower House, sometimes re-worked; for example, a frontage from McConnochie House, a cylindrical tower and conical roof from Castell Coch, and fireplaces from Cardiff Castle.

The exterior is of red brick with stone dressings and the roof in grey slate in diminishing courses, with many stained-glass windows. The lavish interior decorations were carried out by a large team of artists and craftsmen over several years, and were still unfinished when Burges died. When completed, the house was well received and became influential; in the 1893 survey of the architecture of the previous 50 years, it was the only private townhouse included.

The house is now owned by Jimmy Page (Led Zeppelin's guitarist), who bought it from the Irish actor Richard Harris in 1974. Mr Page is a Burges enthusiast and reportedly outbid David Bowie to buy the Tower House. Jimmy Page reputedly has (or had) an interest in the occult, and the house's themed rooms apparently play to that, including an astrology hall with signs of the zodiac painted on the ceiling. (On a lighter magical note, Richard Harris went on to become the first Professor Dumbledore in the *Harry Potter* films.)

The filmmaker Kenneth Anger lived in Page's basement at the Tower House while he was editing the film *Lucifer Rising*, and many Led Zeppelin songs were composed in the music room. As a result, it has become something of a place of pilgrimage for fans of Led Zeppelin, cult films and the occult.

AT A GLANCE

Address: 12 Holland Park Rd, W14 8LZ (020-7602 3316, rbkc.gov.uk/
museums/leighton-house).

Opening hours: See website for opening times.

Cost: See the website for entrance fees. Private group tours (10-30
people) can also be arranged.

Transport: High Street Kensington tube.

Lord Leighton

LEIGHTON HOUSE MUSEUM

This unjustly obscure museum on the edge of Holland Park occupies the former home of painter and sculptor Frederic, Lord Leighton (1830-1896). It's one of the 19th century's most remarkable buildings; from the outside it's elegant rather than striking, but it contains one of London's most original interiors.

Leighton was associated with the Pre-Raphaelite Brotherhood (although he later looked to contrast with them) and his work depicted biblical, classical and historical subjects. He's most famous for his painting *Flaming June* and has the dubious distinction of being the bearer of the shortest-lived peerage in history: he died the day after the patent creating him Baron Leighton and, as he was unmarried, his Barony expired with him.

The first part of the house was designed in 1864 by George Aitchison and resembles an Italianate villa. It's of red Suffolk brick with Caen Stone dressings in a restrained classical style. Subsequently, the building was extended over 30 years by Aitchison, to create a private art palace for Leighton. The house's centrepiece is a remarkable two-storey Arab Hall, designed to display Leighton's priceless collection of over 1,000 Islamic tiles, dating from the 13th to 17th centuries, collected during his trips to the Middle East.

The interior of this pseudo-Islamic court provides a stunning impression of the Orient, including a dome and a fountain. It has featured as a set in a number of films and television programmes, including *Brazil*, *Nicholas Nickleby* and *Spooks*, and in music videos for *Golden Brown* by The Stranglers and *Gold* by Spandau Ballet. These song titles give an indication of how opulent the interior is throughout the house, with gilded ceilings, peacock blue tiles, red walls, intricate black woodwork and much more. It has been described as one of London's most bizarre and magical interiors.

With all this architectural and decorative finery it would be easy to overlook the permanent collection. That would be a pity, as there are works by various members of the Pre-Raphaelite Brotherhood, including Edward Burne-Jones, John Everett Millais and George Frederick Watts, as well as some 80 oil paintings by Leighton himself and a number of his sketches, watercolours, prints and personal documents and mementos. On the first floor is Leighton's huge, beautifully lit artist's studio, with its apse, dome and great north window. In 2021-22 the museum underwent a major redevelopment which created additional gallery space, a learning centre, new shop and a café.

Linley Sambourne - self portrait

SAMBOURNE HOUSE

Behind the shops of Kensington High Street lies Sambourne House (named after Edward Linley Sambourne), one of central London's hidden gems. It's a unique, beautifully preserved late Victorian (1874) townhouse, classical Italianate in style, with most of its original décor and furnishings. While preserved Victorian exteriors aren't uncommon, it's rare to have an almost-original interior.

Sambourne was a photographer, book illustrator and the chief political cartoonist of the (now defunct) satirical magazine *Punch*, and an ancestor of the Earl of Snowdon, who married Queen Elizabeth ll's sister, Princess Margaret. Their son, Viscount Linley – appropriately, given the shared name – founded a successful furniture design and manufacturing business.

Sambourne and his family lived at 18 Stafford Terrace until his death in 1910. After the death of his wife (Marion) in 1914 the house was inherited by their son Roy, who preserved it largely unchanged (including the furniture and decoration) until his death in 1946. It then passed to his sister Maud (grandmother of the future Earl of Snowdon, who took Linley as his subsidiary title) and then to her daughter Anne, Countess of Rosse. In 1957, Lady Rosse proposed the foundation of The Victorian Society and continued the preservation of the house largely as it had been in Linley Sambourne's days.

The house was originally decorated by the Sambourne family, following the then-fashionable aesthetic principles, with William Morris wallpapers, heavy velvet curtains, exotic Turkish carpets, stained glass windows, ebonised wardrobes and a wealth of Chinese ornaments. However, it developed from this and became an even more varied and interesting interior, an attractive jumble.

The notable collection of Chinese export porcelain, from the 17th to 19th centuries – including blue and white and enamelled wares (famille rose, famille verte and Chinese Imari) – is displayed throughout the house. Other highlights include English tin-glazed wares, Whitefriars glass lampshades and miscellaneous glass vessels. There are also a number of Sambourne's cartoons, drawings and sketches on display.

The property paints a vivid picture of intellectual, late-Victorian tastes and lifestyle, and the tour give you a sense of stepping back into the past and what it was like to be a member of the Sambourne family.

Note that the house is spread over five floors, with steep external and interior stairs, and therefore isn't suitable for visitors with restricted mobility.

Address: 224-238 Kensington High Street, W8 6AG (020-3862 5900, designmuseum.org).

Opening hours: Sun-Thu 10am-6pm, Fri-Sat 10am-9pm. The permanent collection (Designer Maker User) is open daily 10am-6pm.

Cost: Free access to permanent exhibition; fee for temporary exhibitions (see website).

Transport: High Street Kensington tube.

DESIGN MUSEUM

Founded in 1989 by Sir Terence Conran (1931-2020), the Design Museum was originally located on the south bank of the River Thames in the Shad Thames area in southeast London, from where it relocated to Kensington in 2016. The museum encompasses product, industrial, graphic, fashion and architectural design, and champions design and the impact it has on the world, while introducing you to the people behind it.

The museum is housed in the former (Grade II* listed) Commonwealth Institute building, which was designed by John Pawson (interior) and Rem Koolhaas (OMA), who made the building fit for a 21st-century museum – with a striking copper-covered, hyperbolic paraboloid roof – while at the same time retaining its spatial qualities. The museum's £83 million new premises are three times larger than the previous building, containing the Swarovski Foundation Centre for Learning, the 202-seat Bakala Auditorium and a dedicated gallery for its permanent collection.

The top-floor space under the museum roof houses a permanent display, 'Designer Maker User', with key objects from the museum's collection. It features some 1,000 items of 20th and 21st-century design viewed through the eyes of the designer, manufacturer and user, including a crowdsourced wall. The exhibition covers a broad range of design disciplines, from architecture and engineering, to the digital world, fashion and graphics. As part of Designer Maker User display, a wall display at the entrance to the exhibition features over 200 nominated objects from 25 countries. They demonstrate the intimate relationships we have with the everyday objects that shape our lives, including a bible, Coca-Cola can, £5 banknote, rubber gloves and a plastic garden chair.

A restaurant, members' lounge, residency studio, and an events and gallery space are also located on the top floor. On the first floor, a design and architecture reference library is a resource for students, educators, researchers and designers, while the Swarovski Foundation Centre for Learning encompasses a suite of learning facilities including a Design Studio, Creative Workshop, two seminar rooms and a Common Room. On the ground floor, the museum's largest gallery showcases a programme of temporary exhibitions.

A double-height space spanning the two lower levels, Gallery Two hosts a programme of temporary exhibitions dedicated to architecture, fashion, furniture, product and graphic design. The Bakala Auditorium provides a purpose-designed space for a programme of talks, seminars, debates, and public and private events throughout the year.

The world's leading museum for contemporary design, the Design Museum is well worth a visit.

Address: Old Church St, Chelsea, SW3 5BS (en.wikipedia.org/wiki/old_church_street).

Opening hours: Unrestricted access to street. Chelsea Old Church (chelseaoldchurch.org.uk) is open Wed-Fri, 2-4pm, and during services.

Cost: Free.

Transport: South Kensington tube.

OLD CHURCH STREET

Chelsea is one of London's wealthiest and most desirable residential districts and is home to two of its most upmarket shopping areas, the Fulham Road and the King's Road. What's often overlooked is that it also has some lovely architecture, with people distracted by the ritzy shops and restaurants and long list of celebrity residents.

The area's visual interest is epitomised by its oldest street, the little-known Old Church Street, which runs from Chelsea Embankment to the Fulham Road, crossing the Kings Road. It's named after the Chelsea Old Church (All Saints) and is mentioned as far back as 1566, when it was named the more modest Church Lane.

The church (4 Old Church St, 020-7795 1019, chelseaoldchurch. org.uk) is Grade I listed and dates from 1157, although from the outside it doesn't look very old and the present building is mostly a replica of the medieval church, which was severely damaged during the Second World War. Henry VIII is said to have married his third wife, Jane Seymour, here. The interior is cramped but has some interesting features. The south chapel was built for Sir Thomas More in 1528 for his own private worship, and decorated by Hans Holbein the Younger. It happily survived the bombing almost intact, and contains an impressive monument to More, while the American novelist Henry James also has a memorial here. There's a statue of More outside the church.

A stroll along Old Church Street is a visual treat, with its lovely old buildings, many of which have housed the good and the great. Numbers 34 to 38 are good examples of 18th- and 19th-century private houses, while numbers 64 and 66 have attractive '30s architecture. Music fans might want to pay homage at number 46a, which was the site of Sound Techniques between 1964 and 1972, a recording studio which hosted the likes of Fairport Convention, Pink Floyd, Tyrannosaurus Rex, The Who and The Yardbirds.

Writers and creative types have long favoured the area: *Gulliver's Travels* author Jonathan Swift lived on Old Church Street, the poet Sir John Betjeman lived for a time at number 53 and *The Water Babies* author Charles Kingsley grew up at number 56. Rock guitarist Steve Clark (from the oddly-named Def Leppard) lived at number 44, while number 143 is home to the Chelsea Arts Club, a private members club, mainly comprised of actors, artists, musicians and writers.

Thomas Carlyle

THOMAS CARLYLE'S HOUSE

This beautiful Queen Anne house is an atmospheric, interesting, well-preserved example of what life was like in a middle class, creative Victorian home, and remains much as it would have been in 1895. The building itself is older, a typical Georgian terraced house (built in 1708), set in Cheyne Row – one of London's best preserved early 18th-century streets – in Chelsea, one of its richest and ritziest districts.

In a part of London noted for its writers and other creative types, this is the former home of Thomas and Jane Carlyle, a literary celebrity couple of their day. Native Scots, they moved to London in the 1830s and to Cheyne Row in 1834. Jane died in 1866, but Thomas remained here until his death in 1881 (he apparently died in the Drawing Room). For the following 14 years it was rented out, but remained largely untouched. In May 1895 the house was purchased and the Carlyle's House Memorial Trust created to administer it. In 1936 it was transferred to the National Trust, which retains control.

Thomas Carlyle was one of the Victorian era's greatest writers, said to have inspired Dickens, although he's little read nowadays, which perhaps explains why his house often fails to register on people's radar. He was a historian, philosopher and satirist, and his wife was a woman of letters, as well as a renowned hostess and story-teller. They had many famous friends and their home became a magnet for a wide circle of artists, philosophers, scientists and writers.

The Carlyles had a notably stormy marriage; a mixture of affection, anger and jealousy, and they weren't universally admired. Some regarded them as thinking too highly of themselves and Thomas was said to have a tendency to be rather gloomy. However, they made an appealing home, and their devotees have tracked down many of the Carlyles' original possessions, giving the house an authentic feel.

The attractive furniture, pictures, books, etc., paint a vivid picture of their domestic and work lives, and there's also a small walled garden planted with flowers and shrubs that the Carlyles enjoyed (as indicated in their correspondence). Thomas was famously obsessed with noise: he hated it and found it difficult to work with any distractions. As a result, he tried to sound-proof his study, but was only partly successful, as visitors can discover for themselves.

Address: 66 Royal Hospital Rd, SW3 4HS (020-7352 5646, chelseaphysicgarden.co.uk).

Opening hours: 1st Nov to 31st Mar: Mon-Fri and Sun, 11am to 4pm, café 10am to 4pm. 1st Apr to 31st Oct. Confirm opening times before visiting.

Cost: £8.50 adults (incl. pensioners), £6.50 students, the unemployed and children aged 5-15, under 5s free, families £26 (2 adults, 3 children).

Transport: Sloane Sq tube.

CHELSEA PHYSIC GARDEN

This gem is a 'secret' garden in the heart of London, a historic, living museum as well as a haven of beauty and relaxation. It was founded in 1673 by the splendidly-named Worshipful Society of Apothecaries of London in order that its apprentices could study the medicinal properties of plants. It's London's oldest botanical garden and Britain's second-oldest, after the University of Oxford's, founded in 1621. The word 'physic' refers to the science of healing.

The Chelsea Physic Garden's location was carefully chosen; its proximity to the river tempers the weather and gives it a relatively warm microclimate, which helps the survival of non-native plants, including Britain's largest outdoor fruiting olive tree (9m/30ft high) and the world's northernmost outdoor grapefruit. The river also served as a transport link for the movement of both botanists and plants.

The garden has had an important educational role since its inception and in the 1700s became one of the world's leading centres of botany and plant exchange. This role has expanded recently, since the renewed interest in natural medicine. Its Garden of World Medicine is Britain's first garden of ethnobotany (the study of the botany and plant use of different ethnic and indigenous groups) and incorporates a new Pharmaceutical Garden, which displays plants of proven medicinal use.

The Chelsea Physic Garden has around 5,000 types of plant, concentrating on medicinal plants and rare and endangered species. There are different environments suitable to different types of plant, most notably the pond rock garden built from old building stones from the Tower of London and Icelandic lava (brought back by Sir Joseph Banks, who also contributed many seeds for the garden, gathered on his travels) mixed with bricks and flint. This odd construction is Grade II listed and is the oldest rock garden (1773) in England open to the public.

The Chelsea Physic Garden has beautifully-scented aromatherapy and perfumery borders, and a vegetable plot which concentrates on rare and unusual vegetables. It also boasts England's first greenhouse and stove, which were built in 1681. Last, but certainly not least, it has an acclaimed café serving light lunches and teas.

Address: **Royal Hospital Rd, Chelsea, SW3 4HT (020-7730 0717, nam. ac.uk).**

Opening hours: **Wed-Sun, 10am to 5.30pm. Closed 24-26th Dec and 1st Jan.**

Cost: **Free.**

Transport: **Sloane Sq tube.**

NATIONAL ARMY MUSEUM

This tends to be neglected by many in favour of the London branch of the rather better known Imperial War Museum (which is on Lambeth Road in south London). The latter has a wider theme, i.e. the war experiences of British civilians and military personnel, but a much narrower timeframe (after 1914). The National Army Museum covers a much longer period, from around 1066 to the present time.

Its fascinating permanent displays 'tell the ordinary and extraordinary stories of the men and women who have served in Britain's armies across the globe and how they have helped shape the world today'. They're spilt into exhibitions about the army's very early years (dating back to the 11th century); Changing the World 1784-1904, which examines the army's role in the expansion and defence of British trade, political interests and empire; World Wars 1905-1945; Conflicts of Interest 1961 to present (Northern Ireland, the Falklands, the former Yugoslavia, Iraq and Afghanistan); and the Art Gallery, with pictures from 1630-2000. The gallery contains portraits, battle scenes, domestic interiors, horse portraits and camp scenes, and includes work by such luminaries as Sir Thomas Gainsborough, Sir Joshua Reynolds and Rex Whistler.

There's also a regular series of special displays throughout the year, which focus on soldiers' lives, the realities of army life and various campaigns; e.g. recent exhibitions have been about Wives and Sweethearts, The British Army in Afghanistan 1839-1919, National Service and the Korean War. The museum also hosts regular activities, events and talks, including free lunchtime lectures (see website for information).

The museum also has a Kids' Zone that allows children to 'live' in a soldiers' tent, defend a castle from invasion and look after all the king's horses. There's a castle-themed climbing frame, and assault courses. A timed ticket entry system applies to the Kids' Zone. There are also two interactive Active Zones to bring history to life, with hands-on learning: The Victorian Soldier Activity Zone and The World's Army Activity Zone.

Many people haven't heard of the National Army Museum, let alone visited, but they're missing out. It's expansive, interesting and poignant, particularly the personal accounts of experiences by soldiers, their families and the citizens of war-torn countries. And it asks searching, increasingly relevant questions about the consequences of both military intervention and inaction. On a lighter note, there's also a shop and café.

Address: Royal Hospital Rd, SW3 4SR (020-7881 5298, chelsea-pensioners.co.uk).

Opening hours: Courtyards and chapel: Mon-Sat, 10am to noon and 2-4pm. Great Hall: Mon-Sat, 11am to noon and 2-4pm. Museum: Mon-Fri, 10am to 4pm. Confirm all times before visiting. The grounds are closed in May for the Chelsea Flower Show (see rhs.org.uk/shows-events/rhs-chelsea-flower-show for dates).

Cost: Entry is free for individuals and small groups (fewer than 10 people). Larger groups must book a tour (020-7881 5237), Mon-Fri, 10am and 2pm (1½ hrs), £15 per head, including a visit to the museum, shop and café.

Transport: Sloane Sq tube.

Chelsea Pensioners

ROYAL HOSPITAL CHELSEA

The Royal Hospital Chelsea is set back from the embankment on the north shore of the Thames and, as a result, is often overlooked. That's a pity, as this beautiful, redbrick, Grade I listed building is regarded as London's second-loveliest façade on the Thames (after much-visited Greenwich). The grounds are also attractive and have been the site of the Chelsea Flower Show since 1913, the ultimate international event in the gardening calendar and a premier fixture on the London social scene, very much somewhere to see and be seen.

There are few institutions in the United Kingdom with an unbroken three centuries of service and none of them is so close to the heart of the nation as 'The Men in Scarlet', the Chelsea Pensioners, and their home, the Royal Hospital Chelsea. The hospital was founded by Charles II and was intended for the 'succour and relief of veterans broken by age and war', a purpose which it still serves in the 21st century. (It has been suggested that Charles was persuaded to build a hospital for veterans by his mistress, Nell Gwynn, whose father had been made destitute by the Civil War.)

The hospital was designed by Sir Christopher Wren and by the time of Charles II's death (1685) the main hall and chapel of the Hospital had been completed (the first patients included those injured at the Battle of Sedgemoor). The work was completed in 1692 and by the end of March that year the full capacity of 476 former soldiers (pensioners) were in residence.

The Royal Hospital Chelsea was built around three courtyards, the centre one opening to the south, the side ones to the east and west. The building remains almost unchanged except for minor alterations by Robert Adam between 1765 and 1782, and the stables, which were added by Sir John Soane in 1814. The hospital is thus the work of three of Britain's finest architects. Even the stable block is regarded as an architectural gem, one of Soane's finest exteriors, although it's little known or recognised by the general public.

Today, the hospital is still home to around 400 pensioners, who receive board, lodging, nursing care and a distinctive uniform. However, much of the site is open to visitors: the Great Hall, Octagon, chapel and courtyards. There's also a small museum dedicated to the hospital's history. The site of the 18th-century pleasure gardens, Ranelagh Gardens, now forms part of the grounds and is also open to the public.

AT A GLANCE

Address: Battersea Pk, SW11 4NJ (batterseapark.org/history/peace-pagoda), along the south side of the Thames, roughly half way between the Albert and Chelsea bridges.

Opening hours: 8am-dusk, although some gates open earlier and stay open later to allow access to the park's facilities.

Cost: Free.

Transport: Sloane Sq tube or Victoria tube/rail.

JAPANESE PEACE PAGODA

This is an ornate, visually arresting attraction in the often ignored Battersea Park, which lies to the south of the river, facing Chelsea, its more chic, monied neighbour. Indeed, some of Battersea's more aspirational residents have been known to refer to the area as 'south Chelsea'.

The Japanese Peace Pagoda is one of Battersea Park's major landmarks, and early risers, dog walkers and joggers have become used to the sight of a saffron-robed Buddhist monk quietly beating a drum on his daily sunrise walk from his temple to the pagoda, an interesting if incongruous spectacle. The pagoda's genesis dates back to the mid-'80s, when the now-defunct Greater London Council was looking for ideas to mark its Peace Year (1984). Permission to build the pagoda was its last legislative act before it was abolished by Prime Minister Margaret Thatcher.

The Reverend Gyoro Nagase of the Nipponzan Myohoji Buddhist Order oversaw the pagoda's building in 1985, a gift to London from the Order. The founder of the Reverend's sect – Nichidatsu Fujii – who worked with Mahatma Gandhi for a while, campaigned for world peace and against nuclear weapons, and sent monks and nuns around the world to build Peace Pagodas. There are currently some 80 around the world and this is one of three in the UK (the others are in Ladywood, Birmingham and Milton Keynes).

Battersea Park's Peace Pagoda is regarded by the Buddhist order that maintains it as a spiritual centre for London (vital, apparently, in such a large, vibrant city), but although it's designed as a spiritual place visitors aren't obliged to pray, but simply to find peace here.

The pagoda is a striking sight, situated in a prominent location near the river. Some of the best views of it are actually from Chelsea Embankment, on the other (north) side of the river. Made of Portland stone and wood, the pagoda is 33.5m high and has four gilded statues of the Buddha, facing north, south, east and west. They show him making various mudras (hand gestures), which have different symbolic meanings.

A small temple has been built nearby, with just one resident monk, who spends his life meditating and maintaining the pagoda. You can volunteer to help with the maintenance work. A ceremony for peace is held at the pagoda in June, with monks and nuns from various Buddhist traditions in attendance.

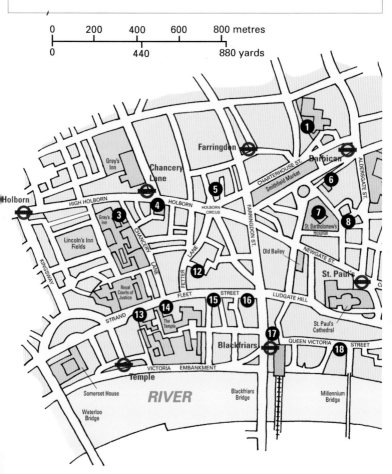

CHAPTER 3

CITY OF LONDON

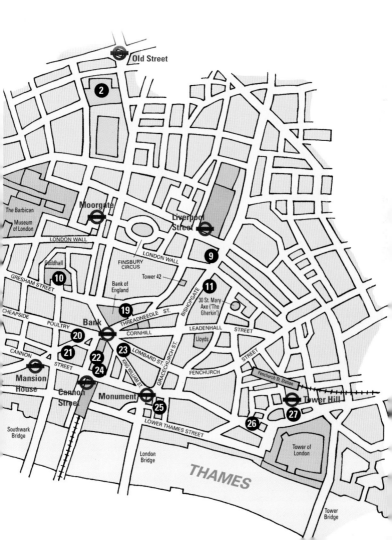

Address: **Charterhouse, Charterhouse Sq, EC1M 6AN (020-7253 9503, thecharterhouse.org).**

Opening hours: **Unrestricted access to the square and exterior of Florin Court. The Charterhouse is open from 10.30am to 4.30pm, Tue to Sat. Tours (ca. 90 minutes) are available daily (Tue-Sat) at 11am and 2.15pm. Booking is via the website: thecharterhouse.digitickets. co.uk/tickets. There are also brother's, family and specialist tours (see website).**

Cost: **Free for the square and exterior of Florin Court. Free entry to the Charterhouse Museum and shop. Charterhouse Tours £15 (£12 concessions), Brother's Tour £20 (£18 concessions).**

Transport: **Barbican or Farringdon tube.**

Charterhouse

Florin Court

CHARTERHOUSE & FLORIN COURT

Charterhouse Square is a historic square in Smithfield, between Charterhouse Street and Clerkenwell Road, in the far south of the borough of Islington, just north of the City of London. It's tranquil, tree-lined and architecturally-significant, and generally very well preserved, despite some Second World War bomb damage (long restored). The famous Smithfield Market is to the southwest (along Charterhouse Street), where meat has been traded for over 800 years, making it one of London's oldest markets.

The square is a fine mix of Tudor, Georgian, Victorian and Art Deco buildings on the site of London's largest plague pit, where around 50,000 victims of the Black Death were buried in 1348, when half the population of London died of plague. The Charterhouse is on the north side of the square, on the site of a former Carthusian monastery founded in 1371.

It was purchased in 1611 by Thomas Sutton, an Elizabethan merchant and adventurer, and became a home for poor gentlemen (a sort of almshouse) and a famous school, Charterhouse. The school remained on the site until 1872, when it moved to Surrey. Today, it's part of the campus of Queen Mary, University of London, and lodgings are still kept for gentlemen who fall on hard times. The gorgeous Charterhouse buildings are well worth visiting. A prep school, Charterhouse Square School, is on the south side of the square.

Television viewers probably know Charterhouse Square best (perhaps inadvertently) as the setting of Florin Court, an Art Deco residential building on the east side of the square. It was built in 1936 by Guy Morgan and Partners, and was used as the fictional home of Hercule Poirot in the '80s television series based on Agatha Christie's novels, starring David Suchet as the noted Belgian sleuth (it was renamed Whitehaven Mansions in the series).

It has an impressive curved, undulating façade, roof garden and basement swimming pool, but can only be viewed from the outside. However, enterprising Poirot and Art Deco fans don't let this put them off, and often arrange to view flats for sale in the building (with no intention of buying, of course). Estate agent websites are also a source of photographs of the building's interior, individual apartments and views.

AT A GLANCE

Address: 38 City Rd, EC1Y 2BG (020-7374 4127, cityoflondon.gov.uk/
things-to-do/city-gardens/find-a-garden/bunhill-fields-burial-ground).

Opening hours: Monday to Friday, 8am to 7pm or dusk (whichever is
earlier). Weekends and bank holidays 9.30am to 7pm or dusk. Guided
walks (90 mins) from Apr-Oct at 11.30pm on Wed from the attendant's
hut.

Cost: Free. Guided walks £12.

Transport: Old St tube.

William Blake

NEAR BY LIE THE REMAINS OF
THE POET-PAINTER
WILLIAM BLAKE
1757 — 1827
AND OF HIS WIFE
CATHERINE SOPHIA

BUNHILL FIELDS

Bunhill Fields is a tranquil, verdant cemetery in Islington, which is intriguingly out of step with its surroundings, sitting behind modern office blocks (meaning it's often missed by all except local office workers). It forms an oasis in central London and is a site of some historical and religious significance and interest. It has recently been granted Grade I status, while many of its monuments are Grade II listed.

The name comes from 'Bone Hill' and the area was associated with burials from Saxon times (perhaps much earlier). It was never consecrated ground and was therefore used for centuries to bury nonconformists (those who refused to conform to the rules of the established church), dissenters and others who weren't acceptable to or part of the Church of England.

The site was part of the ancient manor of Finsbury, dating back to 1104. Part of it became a burial ground in 1665, and by 1854 (when it was closed) it had become full, with around 120,000 interments. Today it covers 10 acres (it used to be much larger), around half of which is a park and the remainder a cemetery.

Like many London graveyards, by the mid-19th century it had become packed, with bodies piled on top of each other in graves until there was only a few inches of soil on the topmost corpse. This was cited as a major cause of London's frequent cholera outbreaks, and the 1852 Burials Act led to such graveyards being closed.

Many of the graves are packed closely together, giving a good idea of how inner London cemeteries used to look (as opposed to the more spacious ones created in the suburbs). Many of the old monuments remain, the earliest still visible dating from 1666. Of particular note are monuments to John Bunyan, author of *Pilgrim's Progress*, and Dr Isaac Watts, whose hymns are popular worldwide.

Other famous burials include William Blake, painter, poet and mystic; Daniel Defoe, author of *Robinson Crusoe*; Eleanor Coade, inventor of the artificial 'Coade' stone; George Fox, one of the founders of the Quaker movement; and Susanna Wesley, mother of John Wesley, the founder of Methodism. The spiked gate at the northeast corner of the cemetery was to deter body-snatchers (who presumably had an easy task, with bodies buried so close to the surface).

Bunhill also offers a refuge for nature in a built-up part of the city, with around 130 trees. During spring, there are beautiful swathes of crocuses, daffodils, hyacinths and snowdrops.

Address: Four self-contained precincts, in a zig-zag from Holborn through Chancery Lane to Blackfriars and the Embankment. The four are at Lincoln's Inn Fields, WC2, Gray's Inn Rd, WC1, King's Bench Walk, EC4, and Middle Temple Lane, EC4 (barcouncil.org.uk/about-the-bar/what-is-the-bar/inns-of-court).

Opening hours: Unrestricted access to the exterior much of the time, but most gates into the precincts are closed at weekends. Tours of the interiors must be booked, although the chapels are often open to the public.

Cost: Free. There's a fee for tours, which are arranged by individual courts and private companies such as London Walking Tours (london-walking-tours.co.uk/inns-of-court-tour.htm) and London Walks (walks.com/our-walks/legal-illegal-london-the-inns-of-court-1).

Transport: Temple or Chancery Lane tube.

Lincoln's Inn

Gray's Inn

Middle Temple Gateway

Arms of the four Inns of Court

INNS OF COURT

Few locals realise that the four Inns of Court (Lincoln's Inn, Inner Temple, Middle Temple and Gray's Inn) are open to the public. This is understandable, as why would institutions that assist and regulate the country's barristers be open or of interest to the average person? However, they're an unexpected delight and drenched in history, with quadrangles, lawns, plane trees and Grade I listed medieval chapels, bringing an air of scholarly peace and tranquillity to the centre of London.

According to the bar council their function is to 'provide support for barristers through a range of educational activities, lunching and dining facilities, access to common rooms and gardens, and provision of various grants and scholarships'. They also have supervisory and disciplinary roles over their members, and anyone wishing to train for the Bar must join one of the Inns.

They have a long history and the term 'Inns' comes from their origins as a hostelry for law students. Lawyers took over the Inner and Middle Temples in the mid-14th century from the Knights Templar (who had occupied the site since the 12th century). Lincoln's Inn and Gray's Inn grew from associations with Henry de Lacy, Earl of Lincoln, and the de Gray family, respectively.

Each Inn is a large complex, with a great hall, libraries, a chapel, chambers and gardens, and resemble Oxbridge colleges in their layout, covering several acres. They're very rewarding to wander around and it's a treat to watch their gas lamps being lit at dusk. Middle Temple Hall (which has a striking double hammer-beam roof) dates from the 1560s, and is the only surviving building from Shakespeare's time where it's known that one of his plays had its première: *Twelfth Night* on 2nd February 1602.

You can enter the Middle and Inner Temples by several lanes off Fleet Street, but the most atmospheric way is through a stone gateway leading to Inner Temple Lane, which pre-dates the Great Fire and is surmounted by the City's only complete remaining timber-framed Jacobean townhouse.

The Inns of Courts' great character and atmosphere have attracted many film makers over the years and they've been used as backdrops many times, including in *Harry Potter and the Order of the Phoenix*.

AT A GLANCE

Address: **337-338 High Holborn, WC1V 7QJ (en.wikipedia.org/wiki/ staple_inn).**

Opening hours: **Unrestricted access to the exterior (which is the main attraction); the interior isn't open to the public, although if you ask you may be allowed a discreet look around.**

Cost: **Free.**

Transport: **Chancery Lane tube.**

STAPLE INN

This large, impressive building gives a good idea of what much of London would have looked like before the Great Fire in 1666. Sitting on the south side of High Holborn, it's the last surviving Inn of Chancery. These evolved along with the Inns of Court (see page 79) and Staple Inn was originally attached to Gray's Inn, one of the four Inns of Court.

It's a Grade I building and is now the London office of the Institute of Actuaries. The Inns of Chancery were dissolved in the 19th century and most were demolished – Staple Inn is the only one that survives largely intact. The earliest reference to the site is from Norman times; in 1292 it housed a building known as le Stapled Halle, which was probably a covered market. The current building dates from 1585 and was once a wool staple, where wool was weighed and taxed. It survived the Great Fire but was badly damaged by bombing in 1944 (it was hit by a flying bomb) and was subsequently restored.

It's a spectacular black and white half-timbered building, with a cruck roof (one supported by curved timbers) and an internal courtyard. One of central London's few surviving Tudor buildings, long restored but looking much as it did when it was built, it does rather cry out to be photographed. Samuel Johnson had lodgings here in 1759. The façade is well known to smokers: it features on the packaging of Old Holborn tobacco, which was originally manufactured at premises off the north side of Holborn.

Today, much of the building is used by the Institute of Actuaries, who've been resident since 1887. The ground floor street side is let to shops and restaurants, which are required to use more understated signage than they might in a less distinguished building. Indeed, they have the air of understated 19th-century establishments rather than brash 21st-century ones.

Through an arched entrance is a courtyard, with some 18th-century buildings, which has long been a tranquil haven away from the hustle, bustle and noise of central London. The 19th-century American writer Nathaniel Hawthorne went so far as to write 'there was not a quieter spot in England than this' and Charles Dickens described its tranquillity in *The Mystery of Edwin Drood*.

Why not stop for a cup of (excellent) coffee in Caffè Vergnano 1882, which occupies part of the building?

Address: 1 Ely Court, Ely Pl, EC1N 6SJ (020-7405 4751, yeoldemitreholborn.co.uk).

Opening hours: Mon-Fri, noon to 11pm. Closed weekends.

Cost: **Free.**

Transport: **Chancery Lane or Farringdon tube.**

YE OLDE MITRE TAVERN

Bizarrely, this quaint old pub, which is geographically in the heart of London was, until recently, actually part of Cambridgeshire (see below). As a result, criminals used to hide here and in the surrounding alleyways, as they were beyond the reach of London's forces of law, the area not being under their jurisdiction. The pub also seems to revel in its reputation as London's most hidden and difficult to find.

When you pass from Charterhouse Street to Ely Place (which used to mark the spot where you were technically no longer in London), there's no sign pointing to the Olde Mitre Tavern and unless you know that it's hidden down an alley between 8 and 9 Hatton Garden, you can easily become lost in the labyrinth of narrow streets. It's a tiny pub, with a front of oak and opaque leaded windows, dating from 1547 (as it says on the sign outside), although the current building dates from the early 1770s, shortly after the demolition of the nearby Palace of the Bishops of Ely (which is in Cambridgeshire and which explains the geographical anomaly mentioned earlier). As for the name, a mitre is a bishop's hat.

Nearby, and also worth your time, is St Etheldred's Church – also called Ely Chapel – which dates from 1291 and is the only surviving part of Ely Palace, which was a seat of power and the London residence of a long line of Bishops of Ely. It originally had 58 acres of orchards, strawberry fields (the Bishop of Ely and his strawberries feature in Shakespeare's *Richard III*), vineyards, lawns, ponds and fountains, leading down to the Thames. The original pub was built for the palace's servants, 11 years into Queen Elizabeth I's reign. In 1576, she commandeered a good portion of the palace grounds for her favourite, Sir Christopher Hatton, and thereafter visited regularly.

The later rebuilt Mitre Tavern had incorporated into its front wall a stone mitre from the palace gatepost and a cherry tree that once marked the boundary of the ground given to Hatton. The tree (allegedly used by Elizabeth I as a maypole) is still in place, preserved in the corner of the panelled front bar. It apparently still produced branches and blossom until the late 20th century, when it was damaged by subsidence.

This interesting, historic watering hole is atmospheric, with a crooked little bar and small-scale furniture. It's well worth making a pit stop here on your travels around this ancient part of London.

Address: Cloth Fair, EC1A 7JQ (020-7600 0440, greatstbarts.com).

Opening hours: Mon-Sat, 10am to 5pm, Sun 1-5pm for visitors (open from 8.30am for worshippers). Individual and group tours (90 mins) are available (see greatstbarts.com/tours-of-st-bartholomew-the-great).

Cost: Free but donations welcome. Tours cost £7.50 per person.

Transport: Barbican, Farringdon or St Paul's tube.

ST BARTHOLOMEW THE GREAT

St Bartholomew's (one of the 12 Apostles) is one of London's oldest churches, with a rich history and interesting architecture and interior features, but it's rather ignored and little known. A priory church was first established here in 1123 as part of a monastery of Augustinian canons and the site has been in continuous use as a place of worship since at least 1143.

It was founded by Rahere (who was of Frankish origin), a courtier, jester and favourite of Henry I, supposedly in gratitude after recovering from an illness he suffered on a pilgrimage to Rome. As he was returning to England, he apparently saw a vision of St Bartholomew, who told him to found a church in Smithfield (an admirably precise instruction). Rahere's tomb lies in the church, although it's actually 16th-century (he died in 1145).

It was founded by Rahere (who was of Frankish origin), a courtier, jester and favourite of Henry I, supposedly in gratitude after recovering from an illness he suffered on a pilgrimage to Rome. As he was returning to England, he allegedly saw a vision of St Bartholomew, who told him to found a church in Smithfield (an admirably precise instruction). Rahere's tomb lies in the church, although it's actually 16th-century (he died in 1145).

The priory was dissolved in 1539 and the nave of the church was demolished. It was briefly a Dominican friary and reverted to being a parish church under Elizabeth I. It survived the Great Fire and the Second World War, and there was some restoration in the 19th century, although it remains London's most significant Norman interior, with massive pillars, Romanesque arches and zig-zag moulding.

The entrance to the church from Smithfield is accessed via a lovely medieval gate surmounted by a half-timbered Tudor building, which displays impressive craftsmanship. St Bartholomew's has a number of different styles of architecture, which some people regard as jumbled, others as interesting, but it's definitely atmospheric and has a range of notable features, including lots of interesting Tudor and Jacobean memorials.

Grade I listed, many City Livery Companies have close associations with the church. And it's no stranger to the world of cinema, having featured in several films, including Elizabeth: *The Golden Age*, *Four Weddings and a Funeral*, *Shakespeare in Love* and *The Other Boleyn Girl*.

Address: **St Bartholomew's Hospital, West Smithfield, EC1A 7BE (020-3465 5798, bartsheritage.org.uk/restoring-historic-barts/paintings).**

Opening hours: **The paintings are visible from St Barts Hospital Museum, open Tue-Fri, 10am to 4pm. To see them in more detail you'll need to take a guided 'historic' tour (Fri 2pm), which meets at the Henry VIII gate (see cityoflondonguides.com/tours/st-bartholomew-s-hospital-guided-tour-Fridays).**

Cost: **The museum is free. Guided tours (90 mins) are £7 adults, £6 concessions.**

Transport: **Chancery Lane or St Paul's tube.**

Henry VIII statue

HOGARTH MURALS AT BARTS

When the governors of St Bartholomew's Hospital (widely known simply as Barts) wanted a spectacular display for the entrance hall to the north wing of their new hospital building in 1734, the renowned painter William Hogarth (1697-1764) – a local boy (born in Bartholomew Close next to the hospital – offered his services free of charge.

He was already famous for his paintings and engravings, which usually had a moral message, but it's thought that he was insecure about his social position and wanted to make a grand gesture. He also wished to be generous to the hospital and to demonstrate that an English artist could paint in the grand historical style (the hospital's governors were planning to approach the Venetian artist, Jocopo Amigoni, before Hogarth made his offer to work for free).

The two huge paintings (one is 30 feet wide) that now adorn the walls were completed by Hogarth between 1734 and 1737. One is of Christ healing the lame man at the Pool of Bethesda, the other is of The Good Samaritan. Hence both reflect the spirit of the hospital in caring for the injured and sick.

The Bethesda painting was done first, in a studio in Covent Garden. It was installed on the staircase in 1736 and the people depicted in the painting *Jesus at the Pool of Bethesda* are said to have been modelled on real patients. The *Good Samaritan* work was painted in situ on the staircase (via scaffolding) to ensure that it would tone in with the other painting.

The paintings caused quite a stir at the time, with their 'figures seven feet high' and they still create a dramatic impression today. Some people, however, don't regard them as Hogarth's best work and find them kitschy, bizarre even, and not quite working. They argue that Hogarth's strengths were his humanity and carefully observed recording of the grubby life of 18th-century London, showing his sympathy with those living at the margins of life – critics don't think that trying to paint in the grand historical style suits this, although others disagree.

Barts is also well worth a visit for its history (it was founded in 1123 by Raherus), architecture and museum; it has existed on the same site for almost 900 years, surviving both the Great Fire and the Blitz. The Henry VIII entrance to the hospital remains the main public entrance and the statue of Henry VIII is the only public one of him in London.

AT A GLANCE

Address: **King Edward St, EC1A 7BT (020-7374 4127, cityoflondon.gov. uk/things-to-do/city-gardens/find-a-garden/postmans-park).**

Opening hours: **8am to 7pm or dusk (whichever is earlier).**

Cost: **Free.**

Transport: **St Paul's tube.**

POSTMAN'S PARK

A short distance north of St Paul's Cathedral is one of the City of London's largest parks (although still small), best known as the site of the poignant *Memorial to Heroic Self Sacrifice*. The park stands on the old burial ground of St Botolph's Aldersgate and is a peaceful refuge in the City. It's quite a lot higher than the surrounding streets, as a result of the rather grisly history of many of central London's burial grounds: lack of space meant that corpses were often piled on top of one another, with only a thin layer of soil separating them (and the top one from the ground surface), so the burial area quickly grew higher than the surrounding land.

The name Postman's Park reflects its popularity with (and use by) workers from the nearby Post Office headquarters. In 1900 it became the site of the Memorial to Heroic Self Sacrifice, which was the brainchild of George Frederic Watts, a popular Victorian painter, sculptor and philanthropist. He noticed that memorials were invariably to the good and the great, and he wanted to commemorate ordinary people who died saving others and who might otherwise be forgotten.

The memorial is in the form of a series of plaques (ceramic memorial tablets) on a long wall underneath a loggia (similar to an arcade or a single side of a cloister). Parts of it are Grade II listed and the plaques are attractive, William Morris-style, with Arts and Crafts lettering, some with lovely Art Nouveau borders. They're hand-lettered and on Royal Doulton tiles.

The original idea was to have 120 plaques eventually, but just four had been installed by the time of the opening ceremony (which Watts was too ill to attend). Another nine were added in 1902 and 11 more in 1905. Watts died in 1904 and his wife Mary took over the management of the project, although she later became frustrated by problems with the tile manufacturers and the costs involved.

By 1938 (when Mary Watts died) there were 52 plaques and in 2009 a 54th was added (by the Diocese of London), the first addition for many decades. It's hoped that there will be more in the future. The park received a boost and increased public attention in 2004 with the release of the film *Closer*, in which a key plot element revolves around the park.

It's well worth taking the time to wander around the park, soak up its tranquil atmosphere and read the plaques (there are only a few lines on each), telling their tales of selfless sacrifice; an inspiring and humbling experience.

TURKISH BATHS

Tucked away by Liverpool Street station in London's financial district is a 'hidden' treasure (and oddity) of ornate architecture and one of London's most unusual buildings. It did well to survive the bombs of the Second World War, but perhaps even better to survive the onslaught of 20th-century office development which swept over this part of London, some of it interesting, most of it bland.

The building was constructed in 1895 for Henry and James Forder Nevill (for their company, Nevill's Turkish Baths Limited, which was wound up in 1975) to house a new Turkish bath, which were then popular and common. It was the company's fifth in London and second in the City, meaning that they had more establishments in London than any other company.

The Baths were designed by architect G. Harold Elphick in the ornate and decorative Ottoman style, rather like a small Brighton Pavilion, with touches of the Alhambra. The design and decoration were much admired at the time. Architectural journals praised the overall decorative scheme and the quality of the fittings, and also the imaginative way in which a modest plot was utilised.

All sorts of baths, treatments and cures were offered to the discerning Victorian gentleman (this establishment probably wasn't open to women) in so-called Turkish baths, including showers, hot-air baths, as well as perfumed vapour, Russian vapour, Vichy and sulphur vapour baths. There were also scented showers, along with alarming-sounding ascending, descending and spinal douches. You paid 3/6d before 7pm and 2/- after for the privilege of entering.

The baths remained open until 1954 – the number of bathers using them had been steadily declining since 1950 and tough economic conditions and rising fuel prices finally sealed their fate. Thereafter they were used for storage for a while and were converted into a restaurant in the mid-'70s, although fortunately the building is listed, so much of the original remains. It was (appropriately) at one time a Turkish restaurant called Gallipoli, and more recently a Ciro's Pomodoro Restaurant.

The building is well worth seeking out, an attractively over-the-top visual treat that provides an interesting contrast with the mostly bland, functional architecture that surrounds it. And it takes on a new life at night when it and the surrounding offices are (at least partially) lit.

GUILDHALL ART GALLERY & ROMAN AMPHITHEATRE

In 1988, the Museum of London made one of its most significant archaeological discoveries of recent years, when it unearthed the city's only Roman amphitheatre in Guildhall Yard. The City of London was keen to integrate the remains into its plans for a new art gallery (the original was destroyed during a 1941 air raid), so excavations and building work took place at the same time, over six years. It's a stone building in a semi-Gothic style planned to be sympathetic to the historic Guildhall, which is adjacent and to which it's connected internally.

The amphitheatre remains are now protected in a controlled environment within the gallery. Entry is included with entry to the Guildhall Art Gallery, which allows you to walk among visible Roman remains. It's an original, striking presentation and provides a good impression of the amphitheatre's scale, with the aid of digital technology, atmospheric lighting and sound effects. Outside, in Guildhall Yard, a curved line of dark stone bricks helpfully denote the edge of the old amphitheatre, which was around 100m wide and would have held up to 7,000 people (London's total population at the time was around 20,000).

The amphitheatre was built in AD70, from wood, and renovated in the 2nd century, with proper walls and tiled entrances. It was used for various public displays including gladiatorial contests, the execution of criminals and religious ceremonies. When the Romans abandoned Britain in the 4th century, the amphitheatre lay neglected for centuries, and the area was only reoccupied in the mid-11th century. In the early 12th century, the first Guildhall (London's old administrative centre) was built a few metres to the north.

The Guildhall Art Gallery houses the collection of the City of London and displays around 250 works of art at any one time (from a total collection of some 4,500), which have been collected since the 17th century. The Gallery was established in 1886, as, 'a collection of art treasures worthy of the capital city'. It contains works dating from 1670 to the present, including 17th-century portraits, pre-Raphaelite masterpieces and a fascinating collection of paintings documenting London's dramatic history.

The collection contains works by Constable, Rossetti, Landseer and Millais, among others; the centrepiece of the largest gallery is John Singleton Copley's huge painting *The Defeat of the Floating Batteries of Gibraltar*. The gallery also hosts a regular programme of temporary exhibitions and small displays throughout the year (see website for information).

Address: **78 Bishopsgate, EC2N 4AG (020-7496 1610, stethelburgas. org).**

Opening hours: **Contact the church for service and visiting times.**

Cost: **Free.**

Transport: **Bank tube or Liverpool St tube/rail.**

ST ETHELBURGA THE VIRGIN

This is a strange little confection; a rare survival of a medieval church in the City of London (most were destroyed in the Great Fire of London in 1666, but this one lies just north of where the fire was stopped), now transformed into the Centre for Reconciliation and Peace. The church's foundation date is unknown (it's thought to be around 1180), but it's first recorded in 1250. It was dedicated to St Ethelburga, a 7th-century abbess of Barking.

It's the smallest church in the City – 17m long and 9m wide – and was rebuilt in around 1411, while a modest square bell turret was added in 1775. It's Grade I listed and has an exquisite exterior, the loveliest building on the street by far, providing quite a contrast in terms of style, size and age with neighbouring structures. The contrast with the 180m (590ft) tall, ultra-modern 'Gherkin' building behind it on St Mary Axe is particularly striking. However, despite surviving the Great Fire and only suffering minor damage during the Second World War's Blitz, St Ethelburga the Virgin was almost destroyed in 1993 when a huge IRA bomb exploded nearby.

At first it was thought that the building was too badly damaged to save but, thankfully, the delightfully simple exterior was restored in its medieval form. The church was rebuilt to the original plan, but much altered internally, designed as a modern space for meetings and prayer to conform to the needs of its new incarnation as the St Ethelburga's Centre for Reconciliation and Peace.

Full details of its philosophy and activities are on the website, but the stated aim is 'to inspire and equip people to practise reconciliation and peace-making in their own communities and lives'. It explores the relationship between faith and conflict, and is involved in inter-faith dialogue and training.

The entrance is via a side passage which leads to a pleasant garden with a fountain and flower beds. In the small courtyard next to it is a 16-sided Bedouin tent, designed as a place of meditation and peace for people of all faiths. It's described as a liminal space, 'a place beyond and between borders, where unusual things might happen.' If this sounds a bit woolly and idealistic, it certainly offers a haven of quiet and reflection in a hectic part of London dedicated to Mammon. Regular musical events are held at the church (see website for details).

DR JOHNSON'S HOUSE

Samuel Johnson (1709-1784) was a biographer, editor, essayist, lexicographer, literary critic, moralist and poet (and obviously a splendid time manager). According to some he was the most distinguished man of letters in English history. He was also the subject of perhaps the world's most famous biography, by his friend James Boswell. So it's a surprise and a pity that this property is little visited.

The house was built around 1700 and is one of the few residential properties of its vintage surviving in the City of London (there are plenty in other parts of London). It was Johnson's home and workplace between 1748 and 1759, and it was here that he compiled the first comprehensive English Dictionary. Johnson first moved to London in 1737 with his friend David Garrick (the actor), and tried to earn a living as a journalist, writing for *The Gentleman's Magazine*. He was commissioned by a syndicate of booksellers to write the first comprehensive *Dictionary of the English Language* in 1746. He rented 17 Gough Square, and with the help of his six amanuenses, he compiled it in the garret and published it in 1755.

This elegant property has been restored to its original condition, with panelled rooms, a pine staircase, period furniture, and prints and portraits. Exhibits about Johnson's life and work provide an interesting insight into the man, and help place his work in context. The house's location adds to the atmosphere, in a maze of courtyards and passages to the north of Fleet Street, redolent of Georgian London.

It tells the story of a fascinating, contradictory character. Johnson was a tall, robust man, yet prone to ill health throughout his life. He cut a shambling figure and was prey to a range of twitches and tics, which has led to the conclusion that he probably suffered from Tourette's Syndrome. Despite giving the impression from a distance that he might be an idiot, Johnson was very learned and eloquent. He was also a compassionate man, who supported a number of his poor friends in his house, even when struggling to support himself adequately.

After the death of Johnson's wife (who was over 20 years his senior), his Jamaican servant Francis Barber came to live with him in Gough Square, and many friends were entertained at the house, including Edward Burke, Charles Burney and Joshua Reynolds.

TWININGS TEA SHOP & MUSEUM

Sitting opposite the Royal Courts of Justice, at the other end of The Strand from Charing Cross and the grand art galleries, this small, interesting, historic shop and museum thankfully managed to survive the Blitz. It was founded by Thomas Twining (1675-1741), who saw that there was money to be made from selling what was then an exotic Oriental drink, enjoyed mainly by the wealthy. The location was ideal, as it bordered Westminster and the City of London, in a district newly popular with the good and the great recently displaced by the Great Fire of London.

The House of Twining was founded when Thomas bought the old Tom's Coffee House at the back of the site in 1706. He then daringly introduced tea, and in 1717 opened the Golden Lyon on the site to sell both tea and coffee. In 1787, his grandson Richard Twining (1749-1824) built the handsome doorway which can be seen today. It incorporates his grandfather's Golden Lyon symbol as well as two Chinese figures, to acknowledge the fact that tea drinking originated in China around 5,000 years ago.

Twinings is the oldest shop in the City of Westminster and is thought to be the oldest company to have traded continuously on the same site with the same family since its foundation (according to government tax returns). The Twining's logo, created in 1787, is one of the world's oldest in continuous use.

The shop and museum are housed in long, narrow premises. At the back of the shop is a small, interesting museum, which tells the story of the Twining family and has a display of tea-related paraphernalia collected over 300 years of trading. Among the exhibits are a copy of Queen Victoria's Royal Warrant from 1837, old advertisements, portraits of family members, a selection of tea caddies, various quirky tea-themed items and, perhaps most notably, a wooden box displaying the initials TIP. This stands for 'to insure promptness' and reflects the fact that the patrons of coffee houses (which is where tea was first drunk in Britain) would drop a penny or two into the box, to encourage quick service; hence the origin of the word 'tip'.

This small gem is often overlooked, except by those wanting to buy tea, but it's well worth seeking out as it tells the story of what has become engrained in the image of the British across the world: tea drinking. You can also taste a range of different teas, free of charge, and indulge in a range of Tea Experiences and Masterclasses.

AT A GLANCE

Address: 22 Fleet St, EC4Y 1AA (020-7353 8570, greeneking-pubs. co.uk/pubs/greater-london/ye-olde-cock-tavern).

Opening hours: Tue-Sat, noon to 11pm.

Cost: Free.

Transport: Temple tube.

YE OLDE COCK TAVERN

The Ye Olde Cock Tavern (Grade II listed) dates from 1549 and has the narrowest frontage of any pub in London. It was originally known as Ye Cock and Bottle and was on the north side of Fleet Street, but has been on its existing site since 1887. It was allegedly frequented by famous figures such as Samuel Pepys, Dr Johnson, Charles Dickens and Alfred Tennyson (as were – apparently – half the pubs in London!). There's a story about the sighting of an apparition in 1984, when a young woman working at the pub encountered a smiling disembodied head at the rear of the building. It was said to have been identified as belonging to the Irish poet, physician and writer, Oliver Goldsmith (ca. 1727-1774), who was buried at Temple Church which is located behind the current pub.

> There's a story about the sighting of an apparition in 1984, when a young woman working at the pub encountered a smiling disembodied head at the rear of the building. It was said to have been identified as belonging to the Irish poet, physician and writer, Oliver Goldsmith (ca. 1727-1774), who was buried at Temple Church which is located behind the current pub.

Originally constructed before the 17th century, it was rebuilt on the other side of the road in 1887 when the Law Courts branch of the Bank of England (which later reverted to a pub again!) replaced it. Much of its interior was dismantled and installed in the new building, including the cock, fireplace and its 17th-century oak over mantle (on the first floor), which was allegedly the work of master carver Grinling Gibbons (1648-1721), who carved wood and stone decorations for many royal houses including Windsor Castle, Hampton Court Palace and Kensington Palace. However, in the '90s a fire broke out and destroyed many of the original ornaments, although the building has since been restored using photographs.

Today the Cock is a Greene King pub, offering a range of cask ales and traditional pub grub such as cod, chips and mushy peas, bangers & mash and roast of the day, plus a range of sandwiches and jacket potatoes. Vertical drinking is the order of the day around the long bar, although the pub is deceptively large with seating at the back and three more floors of seating above.

Address: At the back of the offices of the international law firm Freshfields Bruckhaus Deringer, 65 Fleet St, EC4Y 1HS. Turn off Fleet St and walk down Bouverie St, then take Magpie Alley on your left and continue until you reach the courtyard.

Opening hours: Unrestricted access

Cost: Free.

Transport: Chancery Lane or Temple tube or Blackfriars tube/rail.

WHITEFRIARS CRYPT

If you peer over the railings into the glass-walled basement of an international law firm off Fleet Street, you come across an intriguing, imaginatively-designed site (and sight): a section of medieval building that has been incorporated into a modern one, which is above and around it; a clever, effective way of displaying old remains in a part of London where space is very much at a premium. It seamlessly blends the old with the new, which is a feature of many of the better aspects of London.

The remains are of a crypt that was unearthed during building work in 1895. It was cleared and restored in the '20s when the area was redeveloped by the News of the World (a popular former newspaper). The site was redeveloped again in the '80s and the crypt – which was originally on the east side of the site – was raised onto a concrete raft and moved to its present location.

It's a remnant of a medieval priory that belonged to a Carmelite order known as the White Friars, so named because they wore white mantles over their brown habits on formal occasions. They were founded on Mount Carmel (in modern Israel, hence the name) in 1150, and were driven out by the Saracens in 1238. Some of the order sailed to England and by 1253 had built a small church on Fleet Street. A century later it was replaced by a much larger one.

The crypt – which is thought to date from the 14th century and to have been part of a much larger development – is the only visible remains of the priory. At its peak, the priory was an impressive size, stretching from Fleet Street to the Thames, bounded by the Temple in the west and Water Lane (now Whitefriars Street) in the east. The area contained a church, cloisters, a garden and a cemetery. When Henry VIII dissolved the priory in the 16th century, he gave most of the land to his doctor, William Butte, and his armourer.

Subsequently, the buildings soon fell into disrepair. Then developers moved in and filled the area with cheap housing. By the 1830s, when Charles Dickens wrote about it, Whitefriars had developed a seedy reputation as a place for criminals and drunks. This seems appropriate, as the priory's crypt had originally acted as a sanctuary for medieval murderers, prostitutes and thieves.

Address: Fleet St, EC4Y 8AU (020-7427 0133, stbrides.com).

Opening hours: Mon-Fri, 8am to 5pm; Sat 10am to 3.30pm, Sun 10am to 6.30pm. Guided tours (90 mins) Tuesdays at 2.15pm (see website for dates – booking isn't necessary).

Cost: Free. Guided tours £6 per head.

Transport: St Paul's tube.

ST BRIDE'S CHURCH

As with many churches in the City of London, St Bride's is built on land that was used by the Romans (and probably those who came before them, as the Romans often built on existing sites). The church's crypt museum includes a Roman pavement and there's evidence of a building from the 2nd century AD, making this the location of some of London's earliest known Roman remains.

It's also one of London's oldest church sites, probably dating to a Middle Saxon conversion in the 7th century, perhaps even founded by St Bridget in the 6th century. The current church is the eighth on the site and was built by Sir Christopher Wren from 1672 to replace the 11th-century Norman church destroyed in the Great Fire in 1666 (which is thought to have destroyed 87 City churches – St Bride's was one of 51 that were rebuilt).

Set back from Fleet Street, the church has an air of peace about it, appropriate for this historical and rather beautiful building. It's a striking sight, Grade I listed and with Wren's tallest spire at 226ft. The tiered spire is said to have inspired the shape of modern wedding cakes. William Rich, a pastry cook who was based on nearby Ludgate Hill, apparently gazed at St Bride's and its steeple every day from his window and got the idea to use it as the design for a cake.

The church's long and interesting history is documented in the large crypt museum, which as well as the Roman archaeological remains, tells the story of the seven previous churches. Although the bomb damage the church suffered during the Second World War destroyed much of Wren's church (thankfully the glorious steeple was spared), it also opened up the crypt and revealed the substantial Roman remains as well as over 200 (named) skeletons buried between 1740 and 1852, which provided valuable scientific material.

As befits its location in Fleet Street, the church has a long association with men of letters, notably the press (it's been called the spiritual home of printing and the media – appropriately, the splendidly-named Wynkyn de Worde set up a printing press in the churchyard in 1500). And Samuel Pepys, who was born in nearby Salisbury Court, was baptised here.

THE BLACK FRIAR PUB

This narrow, wedge-shaped, Grade II listed pub is situated up against the railway line at Blackfriars, its shape resembling a slab of cheese or an iron. It wouldn't look so distinctive if all the buildings that used to surround it were still in place. The pub was built in 1875 near the site of a 13th-century Dominican Priory, which gives the area its name, and was the inspiration for the pub's design. In the '60s, John Betjeman (poet laureate, later Sir John) led a campaign to save the Black Friar from demolition, and thank goodness he did – no other London pub resembles it.

On the exterior, the pub's name is displayed in mosaic tiles and a statue of a large, laughing friar stands above the main door. It's an attractive, interesting façade, which was decorated by Henry Pool in 1903, but it's the interior of the pub that makes it truly extraordinary and well worth visiting (remodelled by H. Fuller Clark). It's decidedly ecclesiastical in design, resembling an ornate church or a mini cathedral, with a strong Art Nouveau character. Both Pool and Clark were closely associated with the Arts and Crafts movement, and this building argues against the prevailing idea that the movement was all rather earnest.

Work on the interior began in 1904, with sculptors Nathaniel Hitch, Frederick T. Callcott and Henry Pool contributing. Every surface is decorated – in marble, mosaic, bas-reliefs and sculptures – often religiously themed. The walls are decorated in cream, green or red marble, with illustrations of jolly monks; some sing and play instruments, some pick apples and grapes, others gather fish and eels for their meatless days, and one is about to boil an egg.

Various plaques on the walls carry words of so-called wisdom, such as 'Haste is Slow', 'Wisdom is Rare', 'Finery is Foolery', 'Industry is All' and 'Don't Advertise – Tell a Gossip'. The light fittings are carved wooden monks carrying yokes on their shoulders, from which the lights hang. There's a marble bar and, crowning it all, a vaulted mosaic ceiling.

As if all this wasn't enough, the pub also offers decent beer and food, with the pies especially recommended. However, it gets crowded during peak times, notably during the City lunch hour, although by 2.30pm the crowds dissipate and you have the time and space to inspect this extraordinary pub.

ST BENET'S CHURCH

This small, beautiful building is almost square and resembles a Dutch country church. Much of the exterior and interior are as Sir Christopher Wren designed them over 300 years ago, and the church is a notably fine example of his work. There's been a church on the site since 1111, dedicated to St Benet (or Benedict), but the land has been occupied for much longer – excavations under Paul's Wharf revealed Roman foundations.

St Benet's (or the Guild Church of St Benet) is soaked in history, both literary and regal: Shakespeare referred to it in Twelfth Night, while it's thought that Anne Boleyn and Lady Jane Grey received their last rites here on their way to execution at the Tower of London. Since 1555, it's been the church of the College of Arms, whose headquarters are across the road. The College grants heraldic arms to those deemed worthy to bear them and many officers of the arms are buried here. In 1652, the noted architect and inventor Inigo Jones was buried at St Benet's, but in 1666 the church was destroyed in the Great Fire of London.

It was rebuilt by Sir Christopher Wren, opening in 1685, and is the only unaltered Wren church in the City. Charles II had a special door at the side of the building and a private room from which he could take part in services. The Stuart arms above the west door mark the vantage point from which the King observed proceedings below. St Benet's is Grade I listed and one of only four churches in the City that escaped bomb damage in the Blitz. It's built of red and blue bricks with carved stone garlands over the windows, and has a hipped roof on the north side. The graceful tower is surmounted by a dome and cupola, topped by a ball and weather vane, while the interior has Corinthian columns and a beautiful altarpiece.

Now also known as St Benet's Welsh Church (hence the website address), the Welsh connection dates from 1879 when Queen Victoria granted Welsh Anglicans the right to worship here in perpetuity in their own language (they had petitioned the Queen to be allowed to use the church, after it was – foolishly – scheduled for demolition in the 1870s). This has continued every Sunday since and the website has a Welsh as well as an English version.

AT A GLANCE

Address: Batholomew Lane, EC2R 8AH (020-7601 5545, bankofengland.
co.uk/museum).

Opening hours: See website for opening hours.

Cost: Free.

Transport: Bank tube.

BANK OF ENGLAND MUSEUM

At first glance, the prospect of visiting a display about the Bank of England (or the bank of anywhere) doesn't necessarily set the juices flowing, but it's a fascinating (and free) museum. It's of interest not simply to those who follow the world of finance but also to anyone with an interest in social history, politics and (strangely) classic children's literature.

Housed in a replica of the 18th-century bank designed by Sir John Soane (the current building is 20th-century), the museum tells the story of the Bank of England from its foundation in 1694 to its current role as the UK's central bank, setting interest rates, controlling inflation, issuing banknotes and working to maintain a stable financial system. Audio and computer presentations explain the bank's modern responsibilities.

Displays include Roman and modern gold bars (you can test the weight of a gold bar – 28lbs, i.e. reassuringly heavy), and pikes and muskets once used to defend the bank. There are collections of banknotes and coins dating back to the 17th century (you'll learn, among many other things, that illustrations of the monarch didn't appear on banknotes until 1960); a wide range of books and documents; a small but interesting collection of furniture (some of it designed by Sir John Soane); pictures, cartoons and photographs; a small but historically significant silver collection; and statues and a range of other artefacts, mostly associated with the business of banking.

There's also a permanent display about Kenneth Grahame (author of *The Wind in the Willows*), who worked at the bank for 30 years and rose to become its Secretary from 1898 to 1908. The display was opened in 2008 to mark the 100th anniversary of the publication of his famous book and includes his dramatic resignation letter, submitted four months before publication, citing mental pressures as the reason for his resignation. There are also letters from the bank's doctor, which give a rather different assessment of Grahame's mental health. The display includes details of how Grahame thwarted an attempted robbery in 1903 by an armed man who shot at him three times and who was later certified insane. Grahame managed to lock the man in the bank's waiting room.

Special exhibitions and events take place throughout the year at the museum, often including items that aren't usually on display. Free talks are also arranged, which must be booked (see website for details).

Address: **1 Poultry, EC2R 8EJ.**

Opening hours: **Unrestricted access to the exterior. The restaurant at the top of the building – Coq d'Argent (020-7395 5000, coqdargent. co.uk) – enjoys excellent views from its rooftop terraces and garden.**

Cost: **Free to view the exterior.**

Transport: **Bank tube.**

NUMBER 1 POULTRY

Like many buildings in The City, No. 1 Poultry is sometimes overshadowed by brash, newer arrivals, notably the Lloyds of London building and The Gherkin. But it's well worth anybody's attention, being one of the most significant and successful postmodern buildings in London. (Postmodernism is a movement away from the modernist viewpoint, holding that realities are plural or relative. In postmodern architecture, styles collide, form is adopted for its own sake, and there are references to other buildings and structures.)

It's a wedge-shaped office and retail building, designed by James Stirling (1926-92), who was one of the most important and influential architects of the second half of the 20th century. The building was completed in 1997, five years after Stirling's death and almost 20 years after it was designed, i.e. after postmodernism's heyday, so its reception among critics wasn't universally positive. But many like its strong personality and see it as symbolic of contemporary London. It's certainly an interesting shape, resembling a ship.

The building is clad in pink and yellow limestone, fixed in stripes and blocks of colour. The exterior has a series of 'punched-out' circles, squares and triangles. As is typical with postmodern buildings, the imagery is reference-rich. The turret is like a submarine conning tower, while the glazed two-sided clock resembles the Fascist-era central post office in Naples, while the building also alludes to the Victorian structure that formerly occupied the site. The interior atrium has bright colour play, a typical feature of Stirling's buildings.

The building of Number 1 Poultry necessitated the demolition of a 19th-century listed building, which had been occupied by jewellers Mappin & Webb. This was opposed (unsuccessfully), but the redevelopment allowed the Museum of London to undertake a major archaeological excavation of the site. It made a number of significant discoveries, including a wooden drain along a main Roman road, dated to 47AD, which suggests this as the date for the founding of Roman London. Mosaic floors, evidence of Roman buildings, and Saxon features were also found.

The restaurant on the roof of Number 1 Poultry has a terrace and roof gardens, which afford diners fine views of St Pauls, Mansion House, Monument and the Bank of England.

Bloomberg European HQ

Marble Relief of Mithras (at the Museum of London)

LONDON MITHRAEUM

Certain clouds have a silver lining (however small), and that was the case with the London Blitz during the Second World War: the devastation wrought by German bombing raids revealed a number of hitherto unknown Roman sites, which were excavated between the late '40s and the '60s, as redevelopment and rebuilding took place.

The most notable Roman discovery in the City of London was the Temple of Mithras (aka the London Mithraeum), uncovered during rebuilding work in 1954. It originally stood on the east bank of the now covered river Walbrook, one of Roman London's most important sources of fresh water. The temple was excavated by W. F. Grimes, director of the Museum of London, and the dig attracted great public interest with crowds of up to 30,000 at times.

The site was due to be built on, so the whole temple was uprooted and moved down the road to Temple Court, Queen Victoria Street, where its remains were reassembled for public display. When Bloomberg purchased Walbrook Square it was decided to restore the Mithraeum to its original site as part of their new European HQ (voted the UK's best new building 2018 by the Royal Institute of British Architects). The new site re-opened to the public in 2018, and is 7 metres (23ft) below the modern street level occupying part of an exhibition space beneath the Bloomberg building.

The temple is mid-3rd century, dedicated to the god Mithras (possibly of Persian and/or Anatolian origin, although some think the cult of Mithras originated in Rome), who was popular with Roman soldiers. In the 4th century the temple was rededicated, probably to Bacchus, god of wine and ecstasy. A number of sculptures were found during the dig, some of them very impressive, which are on display at the Museum of London.

It would have been a large, splendid temple in its day, 60ft (18m) long and 26ft (8m) wide. The design is rectangular, similar to a Christian church, with a central nave and side aisles, divided from the nave on each side by a row of seven columns that supported the roof. Seven was probably a deliberate choice, as there were seven grades or levels in the Mithraic mystery religion, which worshippers hoped to attain. Little is known about the actual beliefs of the cult of Mithras, although it was open only to men and its ideals were courage, honesty and purity.

The nave was sunken, reflecting the fact that Mithras was born from a rock and slew a bull in a cave, thereby unleashing power and wisdom into the world. And the temple would have been kept dark, to remind initiates of this subterranean association.

Address: **39 Walbrook, EC4N 8BN (020-7626 9000, ststephenwalbrook. net).**

Opening hours: **Weekdays, 10am to 3.30pm. It's usually closed at weekends except for significant festivals. See the website for concerts and recitals.**

Cost: **Free.**

Transport: **Bank or Monument tube.**

ST STEPHENS WALBROOK

Walbrook in the City of London has a long history, dating back at least to the time of the Romans, probably much longer. In the 2nd century AD, a temple of Mithras stood on the bank of the River Walbrook, a stream running across London from the City Wall near Moorfields to the Thames. Its foundations are preserved to this day (see previous page).

There's been a church here since some time between 700AD and 980AD, when a Saxon church stood on the west bank of the Walbrook. It was common to build churches on what had previously been pagan sites in order to hallow them. The church was rebuilt in 1439 on the eastern side of the Walbrook and lost in the Great Fire of London in 1666 (which destroyed around three quarters of the City). The current church was built by Sir Christopher Wren between 1672 and 1680.

It's thought by many to be one of Wren's finest church interiors – if not the finest – and the influential German-born British scholar of art and architecture Sir Nikolaus Pevsner went as far as to declare it one of England's ten most important buildings, so it certainly merits attention.

As you approach the church, you might find Sir Nikolaus's claim to be rather overblown, but it's the interior rather than the exterior that's stunning. Some commentators maintain that it's Wren's masterpiece, and there's something of a Byzantine feel to the interior. It's rich and cream-coloured, yet calm and understated, with Britain's first and best Roman dome, the prototype for St Paul's. The dome is 63ft high and centred over a square of 12 columns.

The church suffered slight bomb damage during the Second World War but was later restored. It's Grade I listed and also has some interesting modern features, including a controversial, massive white stone altar by the renowned sculptor Henry Moore. Unusually, it sits in the centre of the church, a block of pale travertine stone, not so much sculpted as subtly rounded by Moore. Some people love it, but its critics have rather cleverly labelled it the 'camembert'.

The church also displays a telephone in a glass box, which is a tribute to the fact that the Samaritans (tel. 116123) was founded here (by the rector of the church) in 1953. The counselling helpline charity began with this actual telephone, in a crypt beneath the church.

Address: **1 King William St, EC3V 9EA (020-7726 4878, stml.org.uk, en.wikipedia.org/wiki/st_mary_woolnoth).**

Opening hours: **Mon-Fri, 8am to 5pm (confirm it's open before visiting).**

Cost: **Free.**

Transport: **Bank tube or Cannon St tube/rail.**

ST MARY WOOLNOTH

This is the one of architect Nicholas Hawksmoor's (1661-1736, a pupil of Sir Christopher Wren) six churches situated in the City of London. The land on which it's built has long been used for religion of various sorts: Bronze Age Londoners worshipped here at a holy spring and the Romans built a Temple of Concord (goddess of agreement, understanding and marital harmony) on the site.

St Mary Woolnoth is first mentioned in a deed of 1191 as Wilnotmaricherche, a Norman church. The name Woolnoth is thought to refer either to a local benefactor, Wulnoth de Walebrok, or a Saxon founder of the church, a noble called Wulfnoth. The church, including later rebuilds, was demolished in 1711, deemed unsafe following damage during the Great Fire of 1666, despite attempts to repair it by Sir Christopher Wren.

It was rebuilt by Nicholas Hawksmoor and is one of his most distinctive, original designs, now Grade I listed. It occupies a small site, so Hawksmoor made the church seem grand by building upwards. The imposing, robust Baroque façade is dominated by two flat-topped turrets, which give the building a brooding strength. The superbly rendered north wall has three elaborate blank arches.

The interior is small but beautifully proportioned, which makes it seem larger than it is (the Tardis effect, for fans of science fantasy series *Doctor Who*, whose spacecraft is larger on the inside than the outside), supposedly based on the Egyptian Hall of Vetruvius, a 1st-century BC Roman architect, engineer and architectural theorist. It's considered to be Hawksmoor's finest interior, grand and high, with fine plasterwork and original reredos and pulpit. It conveys a sense of calm and space, much valued in this frantic part of London, a step away from the centre of Britain's financial heartland.

The church was remodelled by William Butterfield in 1875-76 and, with typical engineering ingenuity, the Victorians built Bank station tube beneath it in 1897-1900. St Mary Woolnoth is currently used by London's German-speaking Swiss community.

The church has claims to literary renown, being referred to in a famous passage in T. S. Eliot's 1922 poem *The Waste Land, Part 1, The Burial of the Dead*; and Peter Ackroyd's prize-winning 1985 novel, *Hawksmoor*, features a 17th-century architect called Nicholas Dyer (based on Nicholas Hawksmoor), who's supervised by Sir Christopher Wren, and a 20th-century detective called Nicholas Hawksmoor, as well as a number of London churches, including this one.

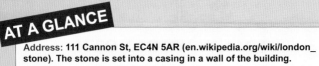

AT A GLANCE

Address: **111 Cannon St, EC4N 5AR (en.wikipedia.org/wiki/london_stone).** The stone is set into a casing in a wall of the building.

Opening hours: **Unrestricted access.**

Cost: **Free.**

Transport: **Cannon St tube/rail.**

The London Stone (at the Museum of London)

THE LONDON STONE

This is one of London's oddest, oldest, most myth-shrouded and – to be frank – least visually interesting relics. And it's almost hidden – practically entombed – in a box fronted with an iron grill on Cannon Street in the bustling City of London, so it's easy to ignore this mysterious, Grade II listed conundrum.

It's a smallish lump of weathered limestone, with a pair of grooves in the rounded top. Recent excavations have revealed some important Roman buildings in the area, and some authorities think the stone could be part of a Roman marker stone, from which distances were marked. It used to be located in the middle of Cannon Street and some say it originally marked the centre of the old city. In 1742 it was moved, to become part of St Swithin's church, opposite. A German bomb destroyed the church in 1941 but the stone remained intact.

Some claim that it's part of an ancient stone circle that stood on Ludgate Hill (one of London's three ancient hills, along with Tower Hill and Cornhill) and was associated with London's most significant ley line (an alignment of ancient sacred places), which runs along Cannon Street. Others claim that it's the stone from which King Arthur withdrew Excalibur.

Whatever the truth of any of this, the London Stone is certainly an ancient object that, for some reason, came to be seen as symbolising the authority and power of London, the heart of the City. Oaths were sworn here and deals made. In 1450, Jack Cade, the leader of a rebellion against Henry VI, observed the tradition by striking his sword against it as a symbol of sovereignty after his forces entered London.

The first written reference to the stone is in the early 10th century in a book of Athelstan, King of the West Saxons. In its list of land and rentals, certain places are referred to as 'near unto London Stone'. It's a landmark on maps in 1198, as Lonenstane or Londenstane, and London's first mayor was Henry Fitz-Ailwin de Londonestone, who served in the late 12th century.

It's also sometimes known as the Stone of Brutus, after a legend that Brutus (great-grandson of Aeneas) and his Trojan fleet brought the stone, as a god, and set up London as another Troy. Archaeological finds have revealed evidence linking London with Asia Minor at the relevant time, the late Bronze Age, around 1100BC.

After such a selection of tales, this somewhat shabby, often-ignored object must be worth seeking out and pondering.

Address: **Junction of Monument St and Fish St Hill, EC3R 8AH (020-7403 3761, themonument.info).**

Opening hours: **Open at weekends and during school holidays. See website for opening times.**

Cost: **£5.40 adult, £4.10 concessions (students, seniors, disabled), £2.70 child (5-15). Tickets can be purchased at the Monument on the day, which may result in a short wait at busy times.**

Transport: **Monument tube or London Bridge tube/rail.**

THE MONUMENT

This, the world's tallest isolated stone column, is seen by many but visited by few. So it isn't so much a hidden gem as a generally ignored one. But it's of notable historical interest and the views from the top are superb. It was built between 1671 and 1677 to commemorate the Great Fire of London and to celebrate the subsequent rebuilding of the City.

It was decided to build the memorial near where the fire began, and it's 202ft (61m) high, which is the exact distance between it and the site in Pudding Lane (in a baker's shop) where the fire started. It's also where the Roman bridge touched land on the north bank of the Thames, and is therefore close to where London itself was established. The fire began on Sunday 2nd September 1666 and was finally extinguished on Wednesday 5th September, after destroying the greater part of the City. Although there was little loss of life, the fire consumed or severely damaged thousands of houses, hundreds of streets, the City's gates, public buildings, churches and St. Paul's Cathedral.

Sir Christopher Wren and his friend the scientist Dr Robert Hooke drew up a design for a huge, fluted Doric column, made of Portland stone and in the antique tradition, containing a 311-step cantilevered stone staircase leading to a viewing platform. This was topped by a drum and a copper urn from which flames emerged, symbolising the fire. It came to be known as the Monument.

It was Wren's intention to use the structure for Royal Society experiments, but vibrations caused by the constant heavy traffic put paid to this. The Monument's main function became as a focus of historic interest and a place to enjoy views of London in all directions from a height of 160ft, the level of the public gallery. It was also put to another, grimmer use: six people committed suicide by throwing themselves from the gallery, the last in 1842, after which it was enclosed in an iron cage.

The Monument reopened in 2009 after being closed for 18 months for improvements and repairs. Visit to enjoy a bird's-eye view of the City and further afield, allowing you to survey towers and turrets of many types, both old and new. But be warned, climbing the 311 steps isn't for the lazy, nervous or very unfit. If you fall into one of these categories, you can save money and much discomfort by visiting the website, which shows the panoramic views from the top, updated every 60 seconds, 24 hours a day, seven days a week.

Address: Byward St, EC3R 5BJ (020-7481 2928, ahbtt.org.uk).

Opening hours: Usually Mon-Fri, 8am to 5pm and Sat-Sun, 10am to 5pm (except during services). Closed on bank holidays. Free guided tours are available from Apr-Oct on most weekdays from 2-4pm. Heritage group tours (1 hour) are also available and can be booked through the church office.

Cost: Free. Heritage tours £5 per person.

Transport: Tower Hill tube.

ALL HALLOWS BY THE TOWER

All Hallows-by-the-Tower is an ancient, Grade I listed church overlooking the Tower of London. It's situated on an unpromising site between a busy road and a shopping precinct, which means that it's sometimes overlooked; a pity as it's positively dripping with history. It's London's oldest church, established in 675 by the Saxon Abbey at Barking and for many years it was (confusingly) named after the abbey, All Hallows Barking.

The site has been in use for much longer and the church was built on the remains of a Roman building, of which there are traces in the crypt. All Hallows was expanded and rebuilt several times between the 11th and 15th centuries, and its location by the Tower saw the beheaded victims of executions (including Thomas More) buried here temporarily.

The church survived the Great Fire of 1666 (which began in Pudding Lane, only a few hundred yards away) thanks to the efforts of Admiral William Penn (the father of William Penn of Pennsylvania), who had the surrounding buildings demolished to create a firebreak. During the fire, Samuel Pepys famously climbed the church's spire to watch the progress of the conflagration.

It didn't fare so well during the Second World War, suffering extensive bomb damage necessitating major reconstruction. But many parts of the old church survived, the outer walls included, which are 15th-century with a 7th-century Saxon doorway from the original church. Three beautiful 15th- and 16th-century wooden statues of saints survive in the church, as does a lovely baptismal font cover carved in 1682 by Grinling Gibbons, widely regarded as one of London's finest carvings, if not the finest. There's also a superb collection of medieval brasses.

There's a museum – The Crypt Museum – which contains sections of a Roman pavement and artefacts discovered during excavations under the church. The church also hosts a wide variety of events, including regular organ recitals as well as concerts, plays and exhibitions (see website for details).

Last but by no means least, some claim that the heart of Richard I (the Lionheart) is buried in the northern part of the churchyard beneath a now-vanished chapel that Richard had built in the 12th century. Alas, this is untrue as it's now known that his heart was buried in Rouen.

There's also an excellent café, The Kitchen@Tower, where you can have a great breakfast or lunch.

Address: **Various locations around the City, with one of the largest and most accessible sections outside Tower Hill tube station, with a replica statue of the Emperor Trajan in front of it (en.wikipedia.org/wiki/london_wall and english-heritage.org.uk/visit/places/london-wall).**

Opening hours: **Unrestricted access.**

Cost: **Free.**

Transport: **Barbican, Moorgate or Tower Hill tube.**

Statue of Trajan, Tower Hill

LONDON WALL

The London Wall is the remains of a defensive wall built around London by the Romans, one of the largest construction projects of Roman Britain, alongside Hadrian's Wall and the network of roads. After the Romans left Britain, the wall was subsequently maintained until the 18th century, a remarkable continuation of usage over such a long period of time. Indeed, the wall defined the boundaries of the City of London until the late Middle Ages. Today, London Wall is also the name of a road that runs parallel with part of the wall's remains.

The wall was built some time between 190 and 225AD, prompted either by the Picts overrunning Hadrian's Wall in the 180s or perhaps as a result of a political crisis and potential conflict over the right to claim the succession as Emperor. It was constructed largely from Kentish ragstone transported by water from Maidstone – all 85,000 tons of it! When completed the wall was almost 3 miles long, between 6 and 9 feet wide and 20 feet high, with a total area of 330 acres. It had a ditch in front of the outer wall which was 6 feet deep and between 9 and 15 feet wide. In medieval times, the ditch was used for dumping rubbish and dead dogs, and became infamous for its stench.

The wall contained a number of gates that led to important Roman roads, the originals being Ludgate, Newgate, Cripplegate, Bishopsgate and Aldgate. Aldersgate was added around 350AD and Moorgate in the medieval period. All these names remain in use for modern parts of the City. It wasn't until the 18th and 19th centuries that the wall underwent major demolition, although even then large portions survived, some of which were incorporated into other structures. Indeed, after the Blitz, some of the tallest ruins remaining in the ravaged City were parts of the (obviously well constructed) Roman wall.

Much of the surviving wall is its core, the majority of the facing having been removed for use on other structures following the abandonment of England by the Romans in 410. A few visible sections of the wall remain (some are substantial and there are also sections in cellars and incorporated into buildings), including at the Tower of London, Cooper's Row, All Hallows London Wall, London Wall, St Alfrege's churchyard, Wallside, Cripplegate Bastion, St Giles Without Cripplegate, the Museum of London garden, Noble Street and Newgate Bastion. Strolling between them makes for an engaging hour or two in this historic part of London.

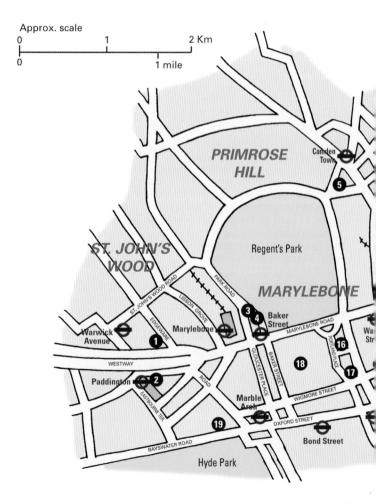

CHAPTER 4

CENTRAL & NORTH LONDON

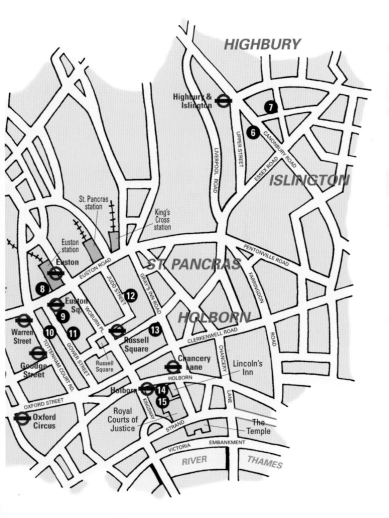

AT A GLANCE

Address: Maida Vale, W2 1TH (canalrivertrust.org.uk/places-to-visit/little-venice).

Opening hours: Unrestricted access.

Cost: Free.

Transport: Warwick Ave tube.

LITTLE VENICE

London isn't all about grand sights and blockbuster destinations. Certain areas – often survivors from a time when the city was a collection of villages and suburbs – simply warrant wandering around to soak up the atmosphere and marvel that such a large, hectic city has so many havens of elegance and tranquillity, sometimes close to the centre. One such area is Little Venice.

The term is employed rather loosely – particularly by estate agents – but it's generally used to describe an area of around a square mile in London's Maida Vale district. Technically speaking, it's the area at the point where the Paddington arm of the Grand Union Canal meets the Regents Canal. But the term – which was apparently coined by local resident and poet Robert Browning, who compared the area with Venice, although the name didn't come into general use until after the Second World War – has come to encompass the whole part of the south of Maida Vale.

It's one of the most exclusive residential areas of central London, noted for being an oasis on or near some of London's canals. Paddington Basin is only a short walk away, one of Europe's largest building regeneration schemes and a rival to London's Docklands. Yet Little Venice is an unexpected haven of calm and beauty, comprising around ten tree-lined streets of lovely 17th-century white stucco houses, with shops on Formosa Street and Clifton Gardens. The area has easy access to Oxford Street, the West End, Paddington Station and even Heathrow airport; no wonder it has become so fashionable and expensive.

The canal is lined with weeping willows and flanked by graceful Regency mansions, many designed by the noted architect John Nash. Houseboats in bright red, dark green and navy blue dot the canal (Richard Branson used to live in one). Some have window boxes bursting with flowers, while others are adorned with elaborate nameplates. Ducks, geese and herons drift languidly by on the canal, which has Browning's Island at its centre, named after the poet who lived nearby.

This tranquil waterside area feels a long way from the surrounding hub of central London and brings to mind the words of the Water Rat in Kenneth Grahame's book *The Wind in the Willows*: 'There is nothing – absolutely nothing – half so much worth doing as simply messing about in boats'. It's a lovely spot for a walk along the towpath (2.5 miles to Camden Lock), while Little Venice itself boasts the Puppet Theatre Barge and many attractive cafés, pubs and restaurants.

THE ROLLING (CURLING) BRIDGE

Paddington Basin is a sizeable west London development, based around a canal basin. It's one of Europe's largest regeneration projects, creating over two million ft² of offices, houses, shops and leisure facilities, including some striking modern buildings, which are worth seeing.

The development includes a new towpath and bridges, to provide public access to the waterside areas, including business and residential moorings. Part of the site is called Waterside, designed by the Richard Rogers Partnership (who were also responsible for the iconic Lloyds of London building) and now home to Marks & Spencer. The Rolling Bridge is one of three bridges commissioned in 2002 to connect various parts of the development. It spans a canal inlet outside Richard Rogers' new headquarters for Marks and Spencer, and is both a piece of engineering and moving art. It has become something of an icon for the whole development.

The bridge was designed by the English designer and artist Thomas Heatherwick of the firm Heatherwick Studio, which works in architecture, furniture design, sculpture and urban infrastructure. It was built in West Sussex and floated up the Grand Union Canal, before being lifted into position and attached to the hydraulic system which powers its movement.

Rather than being a single rigid element that moves to allow through traffic, it opens slowly and smoothly, curling until it changes from a straight pedestrian bridge into an octagonal sculpture which sits on the bank of the canal. It's 40 feet long and made from eight steel sections laid with dark timber to add warmth to the structure and provide a soft footing for pedestrians. The bridge uses hydraulic rams to curl gently open, which sit vertically on the bridge and lift joins in the handrail, causing them to fold. As the handrail folds, each of the eight sections of the bridge is simultaneously lifted, making the whole bridge move until the two ends meet to form an octagon.

The bridge has won a number of awards, including a Structural Steel Award and an Emerging Architecture Award. It can be seen in operation on Wednesdays and Fridays at noon and on Saturdays at 2pm, allowing you to observe its various phases: horizontal, raised and circular (unless it breaks down, which it does occasionally!). The concept of movable bridges certainly isn't new, but this is believed to be the only one in the world that curls and retracts in this manner.

Address: **35 Park Rd, NW1 6XT (020-7723 4400, rsh.anth.org.uk).**

Opening hours: **Office: Mon-Fri, 9am to 5.30pm. Bookshop: Mon 9am to 4pm, Tue-Fri, 9am to 7.30pm, Sat 10am to 5pm. Library: Tue and Thu, noon to 2pm, Sat 10.30am to 2pm and 3 to 5.30pm. See website for schedule of exhibitions, lectures and performances.**

Cost: **Free, except for lectures and performances, for which fees vary. There are regular talks on Tue and Fri (see website for details).**

Transport: **Baker St tube.**

RUDOLF STEINER HOUSE

For the majority of people, this will probably be of more interest aesthetically – as an attractive, innovative piece of architecture – than for the person it's named after or the ideas he espoused. Situated near Regent's Park in an expensive part of London, it's a Grade II listed, unique example of Germanic Expressionist architecture, with a hint of the Modernista, which reminds some commentators of the buildings of Barcelona and Palma.

It was designed by architects Montague Wheeler and built in two phases, in 1924 and 1931. It has curves, cleverly placed asymmetrical windows with stone frames, a coved hood at the entrance and bookshop front, a free-form twisting concrete staircase and other unique details. The rounded door and window frames have something of a hobbit-house style about them, an interesting contrast with the building's Art Nouveau leanings.

Rudolf Steiner House promotes the philosophy of Rudolf Steiner, through a selection of books in its shop, as a cultural centre, and via performances and workshops. Rudolf Steiner (1861-1925) was an Austrian philosopher, social thinker, architect and esotericist. At the beginning of the 20th century he founded a spiritual movement, Anthroposophy, an exotic philosophy springing from transcendentalism (which tried to link and reconcile science and mysticism) with links to theosophy.

Steiner was interested in many fields, including agriculture, architecture, education (there are Steiner schools throughout the UK and in many other countries), economics and medicine. He wrote over 300 books and gave around 6,000 lectures on a wide range of subjects, and it's been suggested that the building was designed to reflect this; for example, the organic, plant-like forms of the extraordinary twisting staircase might reflect Steiner's pioneering work in the field of biodynamic agriculture. (A method of organic farming that excludes the use of artificial chemicals and maintains that there are astronomical – some would say astrological – influences on soil and plant development, notably the phases of the moon.)

Montague Wheeler, the house's architect, was chairman of the Anthroposophical Society in the mid-'30s, and the building is now the base for the UK branch of the society. However, for most visitors the attraction is the architecture.

Address: **221B Baker St, NW1 6XE (020-7224 3688, sherlock-holmes. co.uk).**

Opening hours: **Wed-Sun 10am to 5pm. Closed Mon-Tue.**

Cost: **£15 adults, £12 concessions, £10 children (under-16s), under 6s free.**

Transport: **Baker St or Marylebone tube.**

SHERLOCK HOLMES MUSEUM

This is an interesting concept: a museum dedicated to a fictional character and housed at an address that shouldn't actually exist (and does so only because of special dispensation). Although the building lies between numbers 237 and 241, towards the north end of Baker Street, it bears the number 221B, granted by the City of Westminster in 1990. This is to correspond with the stories written by Sir Arthur Conan Doyle, according to which 221B was the number of the home shared by Sherlock Holmes and Dr John H. Watson between 1881 and 1904, as tenants of Mrs Hudson. (Neither did the address exist at the time when the stories were first published in 1887, when street numbers in Baker Street only went up to 100!) Now the address of 221B Baker Street is recorded on the Ordnance Survey Map of London and at the UK Land Registry.

The Georgian townhouse that hosts the museum was built in 1815 and was used as a boarding house between 1860 and 1936, but has been faithfully recreated as it was in Victorian times, as described by Conan Doyle in many of the stories. Most notable is the famous first floor study overlooking Baker Street. The property is Grade II listed as of 'special architectural and historical interest', and the museum is run by the Sherlock Holmes International Society, a non-profit organisation.

It displays exhibits in the period rooms, including Holmes' memorabilia and a number of wax figures. There are also sometimes 'real-life' figures to add to the air of authenticity, dressed up to play the parts of a policeman, a maid and Dr Watson. As well as a magnet for devotees of the Holmes stories, the museum presents a great photographic opportunity for Victoriana lovers.

Sir Arthur Conan Doyle's daughter Jean (who died in 1997) was against the idea of the museum, as she thought that it perpetuated the idea that her father's creation was real. This 'myth' is supported by the blue plaque on the outside of the building, that gives the years of Holmes's supposed residency. It isn't actually an English Heritage blue plaque (they only put up plaques to real people), but it's similar in design.

In fact, Holmes eventually proved something of a millstone for Conan Doyle, if a wildly successful one. He tried to kill him off a couple of times, but public outcries and large financial inducements kept him writing the stories for much longer than he wished.

Address: **Raymond Burton House, 129-131 Albert St, NW1 7NB (020-7284 7384, jewishmuseum.org.uk).**

Opening hours: **Sun-Tue, Thu, 10am to 5pm. Closed Wed, Fri and Sat. Tickets must be booked online in advance. Public and private tours are also available for groups of up to 15.**

Cost: **£7.50 adults, £5.50 concessions (students and jobseekers), £3.50 children (5-16), free for under-5s.**

Transport: **Camden Town tube.**

JEWISH MUSEUM LONDON

This internationally acclaimed collection allows visitors to explore Jewish culture, heritage and identity. It provides a vivid snapshot of Jewish British life and 'places the Jewish story into the wider context of British history'. There's a huge variety of exhibits and the displays are well conceived and assembled, a blend of traditional items in cases and interactive, high-tech exhibits. The museum also touches on wider issues of minority groups and immigration, which is appropriate in London, one of the world's most cosmopolitan cities. The permanent display is divided into four collections.

The Welcome Gallery is a digital exhibit showing how British Jewish people live today, in the context of their everyday lives. It illuminates what it means to be Jewish in modern Britain, and the many ways there are of being Jewish, 'from the occasional bowl of chicken soup to the full Sabbath experience'.

Judaism: A Living Faith is the museum's outstanding collection of splendid Jewish ceremonial art. There's an interactive Torah display at its centre, and the gallery explores Jewish religious practice at home and in the synagogue. Highlights include a 17th-century Venetian synagogue Ark, magnificent Torah decorations, silver Hanukkah lamps and Passover plates. It's one of the world's finest Judaica collections.

History: A British Story explores Britain's Jewish history, from the earliest known settlement in 1066 to today. Highlights include an evocation of a Jewish East End street, an interactive map exploring the history of Jewish settlement around the UK, and displays relating to refugees from Nazism, including the 10,000 unaccompanied children who came to Britain on the Kindertransport.

The Holocaust Gallery tells the story of Leon Greenman, who survived six concentration camps. It includes poignant film of Leon talking about his experiences (his wife and son died in Auschwitz, while Leon lived until 2008), and there's also a film about four Holocaust survivors who settled in Britain, which highlights the devastating impact of Nazi policies right across Europe and the courage of those who somehow survived.

As well as the above, the museum has a lively, regular programme of temporary exhibitions, events and talks (see website for details).

ESTORICK COLLECTION

Little-known (or even heard of outside the local area), this is a hidden London gem, not just Britain's only gallery devoted to modern Italian art, but one of the world's best collections of early 20th-century Italian art. It's a favourite with locals for its peaceful setting in a beautiful, early 19th-century house and garden café, which is a great spot for an alfresco summer lunch.

The collection's title is named after Eric Estorick (1913-1993), an American sociologist, writer and art collector who later became a full-time art dealer. He was very successful and his clients included a number of Hollywood stars, among them Lauren Bacall, Burt Lancaster and Billy Wilder. He set up the Eric and Salome Estorick foundation, to which he left his Italian collection, and 39a Canonbury Square was purchased to house it.

The Estorick collection has six galleries, an art library, café and bookshop, and regularly stages temporary exhibitions, well-regarded talks and educational events (see website for details). The permanent collection is internationally regarded, particularly for its Futurist works.

Futurism was founded in 1909 by the poet F. T. Marinetti and was Italy's most significant contribution to 20th-century European culture. It sought to move beyond Italy's old, conservative cultural heritage and develop a new aesthetic, based on modern ideas drawing inspiration from machines, speed and technology. Several painters were eager to extend Marinetti's ideas to the visual arts. Estorick developed a passion for their works on his honeymoon in 1947, during which he bought 'hundreds and hundreds of drawings and as many paintings as I could get into my Packard Convertible Roadster', and his collection grew from there throughout the '50s.

Other artists represented in the Estorick Collection include Amedeo Modigliani, noted for his elegant, elongated portraits, and Giorgio de Chirico, whose dream-like works with illogical juxtapositions of objects were a great influence on the Surrealists. As well as paintings, the collection contains sculpture and figurative art, including work by Medardo Rosso, who, on the death of Rodin, was called 'the greatest living sculptor' by the French writer and critic Apollinaire. There are also sculptures by Giacomo Manzu and Marino Marini, hailed as bringing about the rebirth of Italian sculpture in the 20th century.

Address: 6 Canonbury Place, N1 2NQ (en.wikipedia.org/wiki/canonbury_tower).

Opening hours: Visits by appointment. Guided tours are available through the Islington Guides (info@ciga.org.uk).

Cost: Free to view from the street. Tour prices vary.

Transport: Highbury & Islington tube.

CANONBURY TOWER

Canonbury is a residential district in the north London borough of Islington. The tower was built between 1509 and 1532, when the area was farmland and enjoyed uninterrupted views of London. Even today, you can enjoy panoramic views from the roof of the tower, which take in St Paul's Cathedral and Alexandra Palace. The name Canonbury comes from Canons Burgh, as much of the land here and the tower itself once belonged to the canons of the priory at Smithfield.

The tower is one of Islington's oldest buildings, a notably well-preserved Tudor structure dating from the reign of Henry VII. It would be a very unusual survivor anywhere, but particularly in an inner London borough where the ravages of time and the thirst for renewal have sealed the fate of the vast majority of old buildings.

For a time the tower was part of a manor house, sections of which remain, whose origins are very old: it seems to be built on Roman and pre-Roman foundations, and the strategic site has obviously been used for thousands of years. It's also claimed the tower is built on a number of ley lines (up to 24), i.e. alignments of places that are said by dowsers and New Age believers to have spiritual power. Appropriately, the tower is now occupied by the Canonbury Masonic Research Centre, so its connection with the esoteric and the spiritual continues.

It's an impressive piece of architecture, with a long and interesting history. Notable residents have included Thomas Cromwell, who was given Canonbury in 1539 by Henry VIII. Alas, he wasn't allowed to enjoy it for very long, before being executed in 1540, a reflection of how quickly your fortunes could change under a volatile monarch!

The wealthy Sir John Spencer, sometime Lord Mayor of London, occupied it from 1570 to 1610. He was responsible for the detailed wood panelling in some of the rooms and for several fine fireplaces that remain. The author, philosopher and statesman Sir Francis Bacon lived here for nine years, while other famous residents include doctor and poet Oliver Goldsmith and diplomat and writer Washington Irving. Before the Masons moved in, the tower was home to the Tower Theatre Company for around 50 years.

AT A GLANCE

Address: 183 Euston Rd, NW1 2BE (020-7611 2222, wellcomecollection.org).

Opening hours: Galleries and reading room: Tue-Sun, 10am to 6pm; closed Mon. Library: Mon-Sat 10am to 6pm (4pm Sat); closed Sun.

Cost: Free.

Transport: Euston Sq tube or Euston rail.

WELLCOME COLLECTION

This is one of London's most original and interesting (but lesser-known) museums, housed in an impressive, sleek building. It's an unusual collection of medical artefacts and works of art, which 'explore ideas about the connections between medicine, life and art in the past, present and future'. The website dubs it a 'free destination for the incurably curious' and is a useful mirror for the collection, being detailed, interactive (including audio and video presentations), visually interesting, current (including a blog) and full of nuggets of obscure information.

The museum charts the development of medicine through the ages and across many cultures, and explores the impact of medicine on our lives, through a mixture of galleries, events and a library. The Wellcome Library contains over two million items, including 750,000 books and a large collection of manuscripts, some 6,000 of which are in Sanskrit; it's open to the public but you're required to register on your first visit, and you need to become a member to use it fully (see website for details).

The collection is named after Sir Henry Wellcome (1853-1936), an American-British pharmaceutical entrepreneur, philanthropist, pharmacist and collector, whose will created the Wellcome Trust, one of the world's largest medical charities (it spends over £600m annually, largely on biomedical research and the medical humanities – the Wellcome Collection is part of the Trust). He was also a keen collector of medical artefacts and amassed over a million items. The Wellcome Collection displays a modest number of these, including many bizarre items such as used guillotine blades, Napoleon's toothbrush, ivory carvings of pregnant women, shrunken heads, royal hair, ancient sex aids, a DNA sequencing robot and a Picasso drawing.

The Wellcome Collection has three areas: upstairs is an exhibition drawn from Sir Henry's finds, while next door is 'Medicine Now' which contains some striking art on medical themes, including a postcard wall where visitors are encouraged to contribute drawings; downstairs there's a series of temporary exhibitions, many of which are excellent, often challenging and provocative – past exhibitions have included shows about skin decoration; sleep and dreaming; the relationship between madness and art; the history of human drug use and our attitudes to it; and the hidden past of 26 skeletons found in sites around London. There's also a café, bookshop, conference facilities and a members' club.

AT A GLANCE

Address: Student Centre, University College London, 27-28 Gordon Sq, WC1H 0AH (ucl.ac.uk/bentham-project/about-jeremy-bentham/auto-icon).

Opening hours: See website for visiting hours.

Cost: Free.

Transport: Euston Square tube.

University College London

Jeremy Bentham

AUTO-ICON OF JEREMY BENTHAM

This is one of this book's, indeed London's, most singular, unusual objects. It resembles a waxwork but is actually the preserved body (or most of it – see below) of a noted scholar, displayed in a wooden cabinet at a university. Nothing odd there, then.

Jeremy Bentham (1748-1832) was a philosopher and campaigner for political and social reform based on his utilitarian principles, i.e. of providing the maximum good for the maximum number of people. He was regarded as eccentric in his day and his views – which included advocating universal suffrage; the right to divorce; the abolition of the death penalty, physical punishment and slavery; the separation of church and state; animal rights; and decriminalising homosexuality – made him well ahead of his time. He was also a prodigious writer, leaving manuscripts amounting to around five million words.

He's regarded as the spiritual founder of University College London (UCL). Although he didn't play an active part in its creation, he was the inspiration for it opening its doors to all, irrespective of beliefs, creed or race. Bentham strongly believed that education should be made more widely available.

In his will, he requested that his body be preserved and stored in a wooden cabinet, which he termed his 'Auto-icon'. It was originally kept by his disciple Dr Southwood Smith, but UCL acquired it in 1850 and it's been on display ever since. It's currently at the end of the South Cloisters in the college's main building (enter the UCL grounds at the Porter's Lodge on Gower Street). For the 100th and 150th anniversaries of the college, it was brought to the meeting of the College Council, where it was listed as 'present but not voting'.

After his death and at his request, Bentham's body was dissected by students at the university for medical research as part of a public anatomy lecture. Dr Southwood Smith then reassembled the skeleton and put it in a sitting position in Bentham's favourite chair. The skeleton was bulked out with hay and dressed in Bentham's clothes (we're not inventing this).

The head now on display is wax. It used to be the real mummified head, but it was badly damaged by the preservation process (for some years, it remained on display, but on the floor between Bentham's legs). The real head is now in storage at the university. Over the years it was a repeated target for student antics, including being stolen a number of times and used as a football!

GRANT MUSEUM OF ZOOLOGY

In an increasingly slick, high-tech world, this museum has a healthy air of the Victorian collector about it; it's how museums used to be, with the emphasis on exhibits in cases rather than interactive displays, soundscapes and other such recent innovations. For this reason, it's been described as like stepping into a time machine.

It's London's only remaining university zoological museum, with around 67,000 specimens covering the entire Animal Kingdom. Founded in 1828 as a teaching collection, it's named after Robert Grant (1793-1874), who was the first Professor of Zoology and Comparative Anatomy in England. His collection remains the basis of the museum, along with exhibits donated by Thomas Henry Huxley.

There's an abundance of skeletons, mounted animals and specimens preserved in fluid. Many of the species are now extinct or endangered, most notably the Dodo, the Quagga and the Thylacine (or Tasmanian Tiger or Wolf). It isn't a complete Dodo skeleton (none of those exist anywhere), but a selection of bones from Mauritius, where the birds lived until becoming extinct around 1700. The museum has a complete skeleton of the extinct Quagga (which was hunted to death by the 1870s), a type of zebra from South Africa with fewer stripes than a 'regular' zebra. There's also a complete set of bones of the Thylacine, a large marsupial carnivore which used to inhabit Australia and New Guinea; the last live specimen died in captivity in 1936.

Other highlights include a selection of spectacular glass models made by the Blaschka family in the mid- and late-19th century. They depict cephalopods, gastropods, jellyfish, sea anemones and sea cucumbers, and were made by a pioneering Czech father and son team, Leopold and Rudolf Blaschka. There's also the notable collection of Sir Victor Negus's bisected heads, which are striking and beautiful, and have been compared with the work of the controversial contemporary artist Damien Hirst. (Sir Victor was a distinguished doctor and researcher, noted for his work on the larynx and respiration.)

The Grant Museum is also home to a large number of insects – the Entomology Collection – reflecting the fact that insects are the most abundant group of animals in the world, with around one million species. There are some 14,000 of the critters in the Grant, preserved in a variety of ways: some are pinned, some are stored in spirits such as alcohol, while others have been preserved as fossils. Other exhibits, e.g. a stuffed gorilla, a tiger skeleton and a pickled hedgehog, add to the odd sensation of having landed in a mad scientist's lair.

PETRIE MUSEUM OF EGYPTIAN ARCHAEOLOGY

Long overshadowed by the British Museum's renowned, tourist-thronged Egyptian galleries, the Petrie Museum is an unsung wonder. It boasts around 80,000 objects and is one of the world's great collections of Egyptian (and Sudanese) archaeology. It covers life in the Nile Valley from prehistory through the time of the pharaohs and the Ptolemaic, Roman, Coptic and Islamic periods.

While the British Museum's Egyptian collection is strong on the 'big stuff', the Petrie focuses on the minutiae, and provides a vivid picture of what everyday life was like during Egypt's many eras and cultures. Unlike the British Museum, it has the great advantage that it isn't constantly thronged with tourists (sometimes making the exhibits difficult to see, let alone contemplate).

The Petrie is a university museum, named after the noted archaeologist William Flinders Petrie (1853-1942), who was a great excavator and worked on dozens of sites. He amassed a large collection, which he sold to University College London (the third-oldest English university after Oxford and Cambridge) in 1913. The museum is now run by the Institute of Archaeology (part of UCL).

The collection is full of 'firsts', including one of the earliest pieces of linen from Egypt (around 5,000BC); the earliest 'cylinder seal' found in Egypt (around 3,500BC); two lions from the temple of Min at Koptos, from the first group of monumental sculpture (around 3,000BC); a fragment from the first kinglist or calendar (around 2,900BC); the earliest example of metal from Egypt, the first worked iron bead; the earliest example of glazing; the oldest wills on papyrus paper; the oldest gynaecological papyrus; the only veterinary papyrus from ancient Egypt; and the largest architectural drawing, showing a shrine.

The collection is also strong on costume. As well as the 'oldest dress' (the pieces of linen mentioned above), there's a unique beadnet dancer's dress from around 2,400BC; two long-sleeved robes from around the same period; and sandals and socks from the Roman period (presumably not worn together!). Other highlights include works of art from the heretical pharaoh Akhenaten's city at Amarna and the world's largest collection of Roman-period mummy portraits.

The museum recently introduced a new interpretative approach that brings objects to life by revealing the people and places behind them. There are many everyday objects in the collection – including combs, hair curlers, mirrors and razors – and the Petrie aims to 're-humanise' these and show how normal Egyptians lived. Fascinating!

AT A GLANCE

Address: 40 Brunswick Sq, WC1N 1AZ (020-7841 3600, foundlingmuseum.org.uk).

Opening hours: Tue-Sat, 10am to 5pm; Sun 11am to 5pm. Closed Mon and some bank holidays (see website for details).

Cost: £9.50 adults, £7.50 concessions, under-21s free.

Transport: Russell Sq tube.

FOUNDLING MUSEUM

The Foundling Museum's location in a leafy Bloomsbury cul-de-sac is certainly attractive, but has contributed to it being off the main tourist radar. This is a pity because, according to the British broadsheet newspaper, *The Daily Telegraph*, it's 'one of London's most intriguing collections'. The website calls it 'Britain's original home for abandoned children and London's first ever public art gallery'.

It tells the story of the Foundling Hospital, London's first home for abandoned children, which involves three major figures in British history: the philanthropist Sir Thomas Coram (1668-1751), who founded the hospital, the artist William Hogarth and the composer George Frederic Handel. The hospital is said to be the world's first incorporated charity, which Coram established after being appalled by the number of abandoned, homeless children living on London's streets.

The museum's collection charts the history of the Foundling Hospital between its foundation in 1739 and closure in 1954. It's a fascinating blend of art, period interiors and social history, housed in a restored building adjacent to the hospital's original home, which was demolished in 1928. The museum has two principal collections.

The Foundling Collection relates to the hospital itself and the story of the 27,000 children who passed through its doors during its 215-year history. Especially poignant is the collection of tokens mothers left with their babies, allowing the hospital to match a mother with her child should she ever come back to claim it, which, sadly, rarely happened.

The Gerald Coke Handel Collection relates to the life and work of the composer G. F. Handel, who was a governor and benefactor of the hospital. It's an internationally significant collection, the largest privately-held collection of Handel material, including books, engravings, libretti, manuscripts, memorabilia, paintings and more, and was collected by Gerald Coke (a banker and patron of the arts) over a period of around 60 years.

William Hogarth (who was childless) had a long association with the Foundling Hospital and was a founding governor. He designed the children's uniforms and the coat of arms, and he and his wife fostered foundling children. He also set up a permanent art exhibition here and encouraged other artists to produce work for the hospital. In this way, it became Britain's first public art gallery. There are paintings and sculptures by Thomas Gainsborough, Hogarth himself, Joshua Reynolds and many others.

Address: **48-49 Doughty St, WC1N 2LX (020-7405 2127, dickensmuseum.com).**

Opening hours: **Wed-Sun, 10am to 5pm (last admission 4pm). Closed Mon-Tue. There are also costumed tours and walks. The café is open Mon-Sun (10am to 4m).**

Cost: **£9.50 adults, £7.50 concessions, £4.50 children (6-16), under-6s free. Admission to the café, garden and gift shop is free.**

Transport: **Chancery Lane, Holborn or Russell Sq tube.**

Dickens Dream (R W Buss)

CHARLES DICKENS MUSEUM

Charles Dickens's (1812-1870) novels have done much to inform our view of London, and the term 'Dickensian' is still used to describe certain parts of the city. Therefore it's surprising that not only is the museum not on the first page of the average 'to visit' list, but probably isn't on it at all.

It's spread over four floors of a typical Georgian terraced house, although the rooms have a traditional Victorian appearance. Dickens lived here for over two years, from March 1837 (a year after his marriage) until December 1839, and it's the only surviving house he occupied in London. He and his wife Catherine lived here with the eldest three of their ten children, and the older two of Dickens's daughters were born in the house. He had a three-year lease on the property at £80 per year, subsequently moving to a larger home as his family grew and his wealth increased.

This was a productive time for the author: he completed The Pickwick Papers, wrote *Oliver Twist* and *Nicholas Nickleby*, and worked on *Barnaby Rudge* in this property. So it's appropriate that it houses the world's most important Dickens' collection, with over 100,000 items, including manuscripts, rare editions, paintings, personal items and a research library. The photographic collection contains over 5,000 photographs, 2,000 magic lantern slides, 1,000 35mm slides and a large number of colour transparencies. There are also over 500 portraits of Dickens, many interesting views of 19th-century London, illustrations from his novels, and cartoons and caricatures.

The most famous exhibit is probably the portrait of Dickens known as *Dickens Dream* by R. W. Buss, an original illustrator of *The Pickwick Papers*. This unfinished picture shows Dickens in his study at Gads Hill Place in Kent, surrounded by many of the characters from his books.

You can see a 25-minute film about Charles Dickens' life in London, and the museum has permanent displays and exhibitions about his life and work. There's also a range of resources for teachers, students and researchers, and workshops for school groups. See website for dates and details.

Address: 13 Lincoln's Inn Fields, WC2A 3BP (020-7405 2107, soane. org).

Opening hours: Wed-Sun, 10am to 5pm; closed Mon-Tue. Highlights (and private apartments) Tour (1 hour) daily at noon for up to 8 people – book online.

Cost: Free, £15 per head for Highlights Tour.

Transport: Holborn tube.

SIR JOHN SOANE'S MUSEUM

Sir John Soane (1753-1837) was a bricklayer's son who became one of Britain's greatest, most innovative architects, noted for his designs of the Bank of England (see page 111 for the Bank's Museum) and the Dulwich Picture Gallery (see page 293). The museum is housed in his former home, which he designed both to live in and to house his antiquities and works of art (he was a great collector). Soane believed in the 'poetry of architecture' and the house is an embodiment of his experiments and ideas about how light and space should work.

The building has a distinctive, striking front, with a projecting first-floor loggia, Coade Stone statues and Gothic pedestals. Internally, Soane used top-lighting – sometimes with coloured glass – and lots of mirrors to produce an atmospherically lit environment.

He amassed a huge collection of interesting objects and artworks, so many that he had to be creative to house it all, including having panels hung with paintings lining the walls that can be pulled out like leaves or which unfold from the walls. At one stage, Soane and his family lived in just two small rooms, so great was the collection! It's now a happy collection of ordered chaos and deserves to be better known.

Exhibits include Roman cremation urns, a human skeleton, the Egyptian sarcophagus of Seti I, the marble tomb of Soane's favourite dog and pieces from the classical, medieval, renaissance and Oriental periods, including furniture, timepieces, stained glass, drawings, paintings, sculptures, jewellery and architectural models; there's also a library. Paintings include significant works by Canaletto, Piranesi, Reynolds, Turner and Hogarth, including all eight of Hogarth's *Rake's Progress* series.

The museum was established in Soane's own lifetime by a private Act of Parliament in 1833, which took effect on Soane's death in 1837. The Act required that the house be kept 'as nearly as possible' as it was when he died, and that's largely been the case. Soane fell out with his two sons, hence his decision to bequeath his property as a museum. Additional rooms have been restored in recent years and the museum enlarged.

Address: Royal College of Surgeons, 35-43 Lincoln's Inn Fields, WC2A 3PE (020-7869 6560, rcseng.ac.uk/museums-and-archives/hunterian-museum).

Opening hours: At the time of publication (March 2022) the RCS building was undergoing a major redevelopment and the museum was expected to re-open in early 2023. See website for information.

Cost: Free.

Transport: Holborn tube.

HUNTERIAN MUSEUM

This museum might not be suitable for those of a sensitive or squeamish disposition, but nevertheless it's fascinating. As might be expected from its setting in the building of the Royal College of Surgeons, this is very much a medical exhibit, undoubtedly one of the world's greatest collections of comparative anatomy, pathology, osteology and natural history.

The museum is named after the noted Scottish surgeon and keen collector John Hunter (1728-1793), whose collection of around 15,000 items was purchased by the government in 1799 and given to the Company (later the Royal College) of Surgeons. (John Hunter's brother's collection forms the basis for Glasgow's Hunterian Museum.)

Today's museum contains around 3,500 items from Hunter's original collection, with another 2,500 or so objects acquired after 1799, including an odontological collection and natural history collections. The many objects that cannot be displayed are held in the Royal College's reserve collection, which is available for research and teaching (see the website for details).

The Hunterian's collections are rather grisly for some tastes – notably the large selection of preserved human and animal remains, with rows of jars of organs – but they're varied and fascinating, and show just how far medicine has (thankfully!) progressed in the last few centuries. The museum also stages regular temporary exhibitions.

Among the many permanent items on display are a mummified hand, old wax models of dissections, diseased bones, Winston Churchill's dentures, photographs of pioneering plastic surgery, videos of modern operations and the skeleton of an Irish giant who was 7ft 7in tall, called Charles Byrne, sometimes referred to by his stage name Charles O'Brien. Last, but by no means least, there's a display of body parts of notables (obtained by Hunter following post mortems performed at the request of and with the permission of their families), including the then Bishop of Durham's rectum.

The Royal College of Surgeons dates from the 14th century (believed to be 1368) with the foundation of the 'Guild of Surgeons Within the City of London'. There was an ongoing dispute between the surgeons and the barber surgeons until an agreement was signed in 1493, giving the fellowship of surgeons the power of incorporation. This union was formalised further in 1540 by Henry VIII between the Worshipful Company of Barbers (incorporated 1462) and the Guild of Surgeons, to form the Company of Barber-Surgeons. In 1745, the surgeons broke away to form the Company of Surgeons, which in 1800 was granted a royal charter to become the Royal College of Surgeons in London. A further charter in 1843 granted it the present title of the Royal College of Surgeons of England.

ROYAL INSTITUTE OF BRITISH ARCHITECTS' BUILDING

It's obviously beholden on an organisation that represents architects to be housed in an intriguing, inventive building, and 66 Portland Place does the Royal Institute of British Architects (RIBA) proud. It's Grade II listed and was designed by George Grey Wornum, with sculptures by Edward Bainbridge Copnall and James Woodford.

Opened in 1934 by King George V and Queen Mary, the building's design resulted from a competition that was won by Wornum (it attracted 284 entries). With its rich applied decoration and sculpture, it's a prime and lovely example of early '30s Art Deco architecture. The six-storey building is steel-framed and faced in Portland stone.

The sculpted figures on the façade depict the spirit of man and woman as creative forces of architecture. The central figure is by Bainbridge Copnall, the figures on the columns are by Woodford. Along the Weymouth Street elevation, above the third storey window line, are five relief figures by Bainbridge Copnall, of a painter, sculptor, architect (Sir Christopher Wren), engineer and working man.

The pair of massive cast bronze outer doors weigh 1.5 tons each and are the work of Woodford. The deep relief design depicts the Thames and its buildings, including the Guildhall and the Houses of Parliament (left-hand door), and St Paul's and the Horseguards (right-hand door). The three children on the right-hand door represent the architect's own children. The bronze railing designs above the door and the figure of Mercury on the concealed letter box (at the base of the right-hand column) are by Seaton White.

Inside, the most striking aspect of the design is a central stairwell in Demara marble and black birdseye marble. Rising above the stairwell are four massive columns, concrete-clad steel stanchions, each cased with 16 sections of polished Ashburton marble with delicate red figuring. On the landing of the first floor are six finely moulded plaster panels (by Woodford) set into the ceiling, depicting the main English architectural periods. The wide gallery on the second floor is the best vantage point from which to appreciate the ingenuity of Wornum's design.

As well as its obvious architectural and design attractions, the RIBA building is well worth visiting for its galleries housing exhibitions covering various aspects of building design. It also has a bookshop, an extensive library and an excellent café/restaurant.

Address: **Portland Place, W1A 1AA (bbc.co.uk/broadcastinghouse/ visitorinformation.html).**

Opening hours: **Unrestricted access to the exterior (which is the main attraction). You can see a show for free by applying online (bbc.co.uk/ showsandtours/shows). Tours of Broadcasting House are no longer available.**

Cost: **Free to view exterior.**

Transport: **Oxford Circus tube.**

BROADCASTING HOUSE

The BBC's Broadcasting House is a notable example of Art Deco design, although what goes on inside the UK's first purpose-built broadcast centre often obscures the attractions of the structure itself. Built in 1932 eight years after the BBC came into existence, the design was based on an American skyscraper. It revolved around the idea of a studio tower in the middle, with offices flanking it, providing daylight and acting as noise insulation (imperfect, as it turned out).

The original design – by the British architect George Val Myer, in collaboration with the BBC's civil engineer M. T. Tudsbery – had to be modified, as local residents complained that such a tall building would block their light. As a result of the design amendment, the building has an odd (or interesting, if you prefer) asymmetrical form, with one side of the top lower than the other. It's certainly one of London's most distinctive structures; its shape has been likened to a top hat or an ocean cruise liner. Some commentators have been critical, calling it 'this battleship of modernism' and 'a fortified medieval castle'.

The building is clad in Portland stone to blend in with the surrounding Regency architecture. Its blazing white covering and Art Deco profile are adorned by modernist carvings and sculptures by Eric Gill, a British sculptor, designer and stonecutter associated with the Arts and Crafts movement. A conflicted individual, he was both very religious and obsessed with sex (including, it's claimed, an incestuous relationship with his sister and unnatural acts with his dog).

Gill's working methods were certainly controversial. He insisted on working on the statues above the main entrance wearing a monk's habit with nothing on underneath, regardless of the people entering and leaving the building below him. These statues are of Prospero and Ariel (from Shakespeare's *The Tempest*), deemed appropriate for the building because Prospero was a magician and Ariel was a spirit of the air (and radio waves, of course, travel in air).

Despite this, Gill is said to have carved the two figures as God and Man. And his nature rather got the better of him: he carved a girl's face into Prospero's backside and gave Ariel rather large genitals, which he later had to reduce in size. This would be quite controversial even today, all the more so in the '30s.

AT A GLANCE

Address: Hertford House, Manchester Sq, W1U 3BN (020-7563 9500, wallacecollection.org).

Opening hours: Daily 10am-5pm, including bank holidays.

Cost: Free, including temporary exhibitions.

Transport: Baker St, Bond St or Marble Arch.

WALLACE COLLECTION

This is one of London's best art collections, but it doesn't pull in the crowds as it should, which is a pity – except for those who visit, who get to enjoy the pictures and other treasures in rooms that are sometimes almost devoid of visitors. It's also located in an attractive house built in 1776, pleasantly situated in Manchester Square, one of central London's smaller but best-preserved Georgian squares (which is worth wandering around).

The Wallace Collection is a treasure trove of fine and decorative arts dating from the 15th to 19th centuries, spread over 25 galleries. It has many French 18th-century paintings, furniture (one of the finest collections of French furniture outside of France), Sèvres porcelain, arms and armour, and Old Master paintings.

It's mainly the collection of the first four Marquesses of Hertford, particularly the fourth, Richard Seymour-Conway (1800-1870), who left it and the house to his illegitimate son (although he never acknowledged his paternity) Sir Richard Wallace (1818-1890), who was also an important contributor to the collection and whose widow bequeathed it to the nation in 1897 (it opened to the public in 1900). A condition of the bequest was that no object should ever leave the collection, even for temporary exhibition elsewhere, and no works can be stored off-site.

The collection comprises around 5,500 objects and is split into six curatorial departments: Pictures and Miniatures; Ceramics and Glass; Sculpture and Works of Art; Arms and Armour; Sèvres Porcelain; and Gold Boxes and Furniture. The paintings collection includes work by such notables as Canaletto, Delacroix, Fragonard, Gainsborough, Hals (The Laughing Cavalier), Landseer, Murillo, Poussin, Rembrandt, Reynolds, Rubens, Titian, Turner, Van Dyck and Velasquez. There's a fine collection of arms and armour – European and Oriental – plus bronzes, enamels, glass, majolica, miniatures and sculpture – something to appeal to almost everybody.

The detailed website has a useful facility for exploring the various collections and galleries, which is helpful when planning how to get the most from your visit. And when you're sated with culture and priceless treasures, the café and brasserie in the attractive, tranquil, glass-roofed courtyard is a pleasant place for a drink or lunch.

105 CATHOLIC MARTYRS LOST THEIR LIVES AT THE TYBURN GALLOWS NEAR THIS SITE

TYBURN CONVENT & TREE

The Tyburn Convent was founded as recently as 1901, but it's dedicated to something much older (and decidedly grisly) located nearby. It's a Catholic convent, a cloistered community of around 25 Benedictine contemplatives (who never leave their enclosed walls, except for medical treatment), dedicated to the memory of martyrs executed at the nearby Tyburn Tree gallows (and elsewhere) for their Catholic faith. Around 105 Roman Catholics were hanged at Tyburn during the Reformation (1535-1681).

The convent is a peaceful sanctuary among the surrounding noise and chaos of the West End, and in the crypt you can see a series of gruesome relics of the Catholic martyrs' executions, including bloodstained clothing, unpolished fingernails, bone fragments and locks of hair, which are conserved in the cold, dry cellar. Paintings of the executions add to the gruesome atmosphere, as does a replica of the Tyburn Tree. The exhibit is certainly one of London's more unusual and fascinating sights.

A circular plaque in a traffic island at nearby Marble Arch points to the area's long history as a place of execution. It claims to be the exact spot of the Tyburn Tree gallows, a place of public execution from 1196 to 1783, when executions were moved to Newgate prison. The gallows overlooked Hyde Park, where it's estimated that between 40,000 and 60,000 people died, most of them commoners. The gallows were at the junction of what is now Edgware Road, Park Lane and Oxford Street (the former Tyburn Road).

The first hangings were carried out from tree branches on the banks of the Tyburn River (that flowed from Hampstead to the Thames and is now one of London's 'lost rivers', being completely underground), but in 1220 a pair of gallows were built on the site. A Triple Tree (or Triple Gallows) was built in 1571, to a large, triangular design, the three posts 18ft high and the crossbeams 9ft long, capable of hanging 24 people at once (8 on each horizontal beam). It was used at full capacity just once, in 1649, but usually more than one person was hanged at a time. This gallows was removed in 1759 because it was obstructing the road, and replaced by a mobile gallows.

Huge crowds gathered to watch the executions and it was believed that the bodies of the dead had curative properties. People paid the hangman for the chance to stroke the hands of the dead across their faces or injuries. Something to ponder as you stand on the spot where so many died.

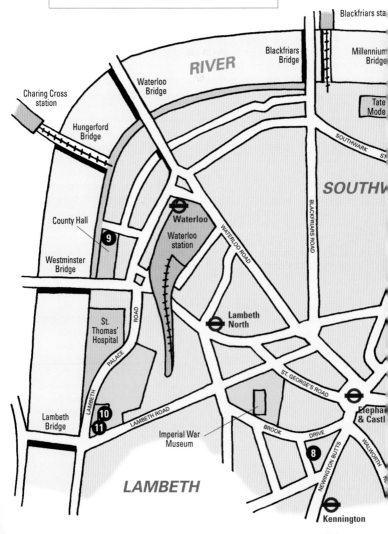

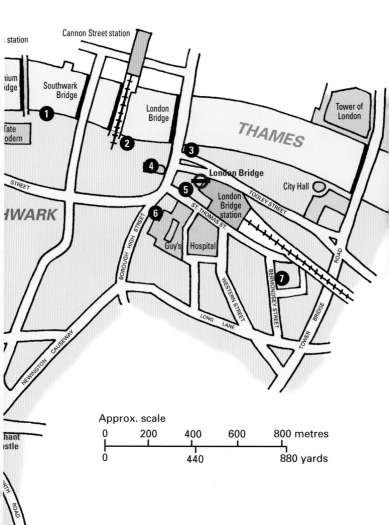

Address: Various stretches of the Thames (see opposite).

Opening hours: Unrestricted access, but generally limited to daylight hours and dependent on the tides.

Cost: Usually free, but you must obtain a permit for mudlarking (2022: monthly permit £42; three-year permit, adult £96, junior 15-17 £63, 12-14 £36). Contact the Port of London Authority for further information (01474-562339, pla.co.uk/environment/thames-foreshore-permit, foreshorepermits@pla.co.uk).

Transport: Several points of access on the south bank from London Bridge tube/rail.

THE THAMES FORESHORE

The Thames has been called 'liquid history', and the foreshore is increasingly regarded as one of the capital's greatest undiscovered historical resources. The nature of the Thames mud makes it especially rich archaeologically, as its low oxygen content helps to slow the rate of organic decay. The foreshore is also London's largest natural space and a wildlife corridor through the heart of the city.

The Thames foreshore is scoured twice daily by tides and regularly by the growing amount of river traffic, all of which constantly reveals objects once buried in the mud. When the tide is out it's the longest open-air archaeological site in London, and much of it is freely accessible to the public.

A great deal has been found on the foreshore, most commonly pottery and clay pipes, but there are also ships' timbers, human burials, Saxon fishtraps and much else. In 2010 there was a particularly exciting and important discovery: the piles forming part of a 6,000- or 7,000-year-old structure, just yards from the MI6 building in Vauxhall (armed police arrived to quiz archaeologists examining the find, as an onlooker had seen them poking around in the silt and mistaken their equipment for weapons). The piles are Mesolithic (Middle Stone Age), and structural finds from this period are rare anywhere in Britain. Tools and Neolithic (New Stone Age) pottery were also found at the site, which is around 600m downstream from a Bronze Age timber bridge or jetty discovered in the '90s.

There are plenty of access points to the Thames foreshore, with a notable number along the south bank. Many have open gates, including at Tate Modern, Bankside Gallery, Blackfriars Bridge, Gabriel's Wharf and Festival Bridge. Be careful and well-prepared before venturing onto the foreshore. Check tide times and always be aware of the location of your nearest point of exit. Wear boots and robust clothing, and take care on the slippery terrain. Keep a close eye on children and always carry a mobile phone. Cover wounds, avoid hand-to-face contact and wash your hands thoroughly afterwards.

Discovering the river's treasures is sometimes called 'mudlarking', following the example of the Victorian poor and street children who scraped a living by finding bits and pieces on the Thames foreshore, hopefully to sell, including lumps of coal and bone (the latter was ground up for fertiliser).

Today, permission is required from the Port of London Authority (PLA – see box opposite) to dig or to use metal detectors and all objects found that could be of archaeological interest must be reported to the Museum of London.

Clink St, SE1 (Clink Prison Museum, 1 Clink St, SE1 9DG, 0900, clink.co.uk).

hours: The ruins of Winchester Palace have unrestricted although they're best viewed in daylight hours. Clink Prison , daily 10am to 6pm.

nchester Palace is free to view (no access). Clink Prison: £8 6 children and concessions, £23 families (two adults and two under 16).

t: London Bridge tube/rail.

Clink Museum

WINCHESTER PALACE & CLINK PRISON MUSEUM

The atmospherically-named Clink Street houses two of London's best unsung attractions; the remains of Winchester Palace and the Clink Prison Museum. Southwark was the largest town in the old diocese of Winchester and the Bishop of Winchester was a major landowner in the area. He was also a power in the land, Winchester being the old Saxon capital of England, and regularly needed to be in London on royal or administrative state business (the bishop was usually either the Chancellor or Treasurer of the King). For this purpose, Henry of Blois built the palace in the 12th century as his comfortable and high-status London residence.

Winchester Palace was one of the largest and most important buildings in medieval London, with a lavishly decorated great hall that was often used to entertain royal guests. The palace stood in a 70-acre park with a huge river frontage, a tennis court, bowling alley and pleasure gardens. After the bishops moved to Chelsea (see **Fulham Palace** on page 203) in the 17th century, the palace was divided into tenements and warehouses, but was mostly destroyed by fire in 1814.

The remains of Winchester Palace gazes down majestically over the street, an unexpected, rare fragment of a bishop's palace dating to 1109. It consists mainly of a tall wall topped by a distinctive, elegant, 13-foot hexagonal rose window (which dates from the 14th century, on 12th-century foundations), with three doors, to the buttery, kitchen and pantry.

The Clink was the bishop's notorious jail (or gaol), in use from 1144 to 1780. It's certainly one of England's oldest prisons, if not the oldest. The name Clink is thought to come from the sound of striking metal, either the prison's metal doors as they closed, or the rattle of the prisoners' chains; hence the expression 'being in clink'. The prison was used to control the Southbank of London, known as 'The Liberty of The Clink', an area outside the jurisdiction of the City that became notorious for brothels and bull- and bear-baiting (it was also home to Shakespeare's Globe Theatre). Indeed, the area's prostitutes were known as 'Winchester geese'.

The prison was burned down in the anti-Catholic riots of 1780, and there's now an excellent museum on the original site, which tells the history of the prison and of policing, punishment and Southwark's colourful past. The museum offers visitors a hands-on educational experience, including handling original artefacts such as grisly torture devices, as well as the opportunity to view and hear the amazing stories of the inmates and the notorious Southbank.

AT A GLANCE

Address: **Tooley St, SE1 2PE.**

Opening hours: **Unrestricted access to the exterior.**

Cost: **Free.**

Transport: **London Bridge tube/rail.**

ST OLAF HOUSE

St Olaf House is one of London's finest Art Deco buildings, a Grade II listed delight sitting on the south bank of the river, near London Bridge. It was built as an office block for the Hays Wharf Company between 1928 and 1932 by architect Harry Stuart Goodhart-Rendel and Oxford Slade Professor of Fine Art (between 1933 and 1936). It now houses London Bridge Hospital's consulting and administration rooms, so the interior isn't open to the public.

The building is named after St Olaf, who was originally Olaf Haraldsson, King of Norway from 1015 to 1028, who was later canonised. He was an ally of Aethelred the Unready and attacked Cnut's forces occupying London Bridge in 1013. These attacks are believed by some to be the origin of the nursery rhyme *London Bridge is Falling Down*. The building sits on a site previously occupied by a church dedicated to the saint and which dates back to at least 1086, when it's mentioned in the Southwark entry in the *Domesday Book*.

St Olaf House is a fine example of the Art Deco style, and is now regarded as a notable landmark in the introduction of a modern style of continental architecture to Britain in the '30s (although it was controversial at the time). Its Thames' frontage bears the name of the Hays Wharf Company in gold stylised lettering along the top of the building. The central section of the riverside façade displays a large relief panel of gilded metal and terracotta, with black granite incised edging designed by Frank Dobson, artist, sculptor and Professor of Sculpture at the Royal College of Art between 1946 and 1953. There are three stylised figures at the top (representing capital, labour and commerce) and 36 smaller abstract panels below.

At first sight, the Tooley Street façade isn't as decorative as the Thames frontage, but closer examination reveals some beautiful features. It has elegant, thin rectangular windows, in sets of three. The name 'St Olaf House' appears in stylised script above the doorway. The door itself has an attractive, understated metal wave motif, while St Olaf is pictured on the sleekly curved corner of the building (but spelt St Olave), drawn in black and gold mosaic to a design by Frank Dobson. At the other end of the building the windows are again arranged in sets of three, this time offset from each other, making them step down, and contrasting with the other end where the sets of three are parallel.

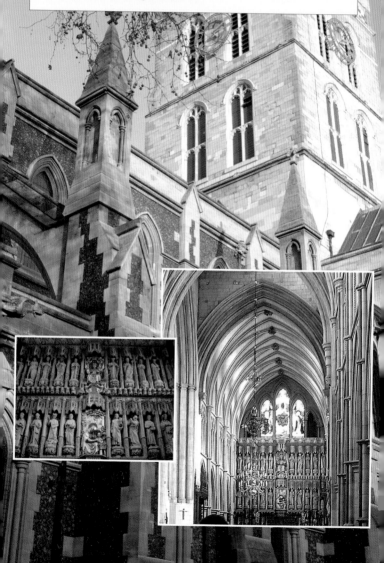

AT A GLANCE

Address: London Br, SE1 9DA (020-7367 6700, cathedral.southwark.anglican.org).

Opening hours: Mon-Sat, 9am to 6pm, Sun 8.30am to 5pm.

Cost: Free. Cathedral history tour (90 mins), adults £10 per head, specialist tours (60 mins) £8 per head.

Transport: London Bridge tube/rail.

SOUTHWARK CATHEDRAL

Often unjustly overlooked in a much-visited part of London (the buzzy south bank of the Thames, near London Bridge and Borough Market), Southwark Cathedral is beautiful and historic. It has been a place of worship for over 1,000 years and is the mother church of the Anglican diocese of Southwark, but has only been designated a cathedral since 1905.

The cathedral is strategically sited at the oldest crossing point of the tidal Thames, and has long been a place, not just of worship, but of hospitality and refuge. It continues to be a form of sanctuary in this secular age; its churchyard is a tranquil haven at the heart of London and a favourite lunch spot for visitors and the area's office workers.

There are claims that a convent was founded on the site in 606 and a monastery by St Swithun in the 9th century (but there's no proof of either), stories which were handed down by word of mouth and reported by the Elizabethan historian John Stow. Archaeological evidence, however, shows that the site was in use (long before any Christian building) by the Romans, who often built on top of earlier settlements, so its use is probably much older. Indeed, the cathedral's website refers – slightly disapprovingly? – to 'Roman pagan worship'. Despite this, parts of the old Roman paving can still be seen, having been incorporated into the floors of the north and south choir aisles.

The site's first official mention is in the *Domesday Book* of 1086, as the 'minster' of Southwark, but it's unlikely that this minster pre-dates the conversion of Wessex in the mid-7th century. The current building is mainly Gothic, dating from 1220 to 1420, making it London's first Gothic church. A Norman arch from the 12th century survives in the north aisle of the nave.

It isn't just the building that's beautiful and historic: the cathedral is also rich in internal interest, including an oak effigy of a knight dating from around 1275, and there's an 'archaeological chamber' within the cathedral which provides glimpses of the site's history, including a view of the gravelled surface of a Roman road that once ran through the area and of Saxon foundations of the early church.

The cathedral is a popular venue for concerts and recitals – see the website for the programme of events.

OLD OPERATING THEATRE & HERB GARRET

Tucked away between London Bridge Station and Guy's Hospital, this is one of London's most unusual museums (and one of its most long-windedly named ones!). It's a museum of surgical history, impressively and evocatively situated in one of the world's oldest surviving operating theatres.

The operating theatre is located in the garret (roof space) of an English Baroque church, St Thomas's Church (built in around 1703), on the original site of St Thomas's Hospital, which dates back to the 12th century when it was part of a monastery. This seems odd but actually makes sense, as the wards of the south wing of St Thomas's Hospital were built around St Thomas's Church, and the operating theatre was sited in the church's Herb Garret, i.e. a place for curing and storing herbs. (Herb storage was often at the top of buildings, away from damp and in an environment that allowed air to circulate.)

The museum has a collection of objects relating to medical history and that of St Thomas's and Guy's hospitals. Many of these reveal the grimness of medicine before the age of science, and make you realise and appreciate how lucky we are to have access to modern techniques and knowledge. This was a time before anaesthetics (which weren't available until 1847 – when ether and chloroform became available) and surgeons had to use quick techniques, with the copious amounts of blood generated soaked up by sawdust.

It was also before the connection between dirt and infection was understood, and before antiseptics. Surgeons often worked in clothes caked with blood and pus, and surgery was only used as a last resort, with patients already weak as a result and therefore even less likely to survive the insanitary, brutal operations. As a result, they often died.

The Old Operating Theatre was built in 1822 and its patients were all women. They were mainly the poor, as the rich tended to be treated in the comfort and privacy of their own homes rather than in a hospital, with operations usually taking place on the kitchen table. Patients at the Old Operating Theatre had to put up with an audience of students, but doing so gave them access to the best surgeons of the day.

AT A GLANCE

Address: George Inn Yard, 75-77 Borough High St, SE1 1NH (020-7407 2056, greeneking-pubs.co.uk/pubs/greater-london/george-southwark, nationaltrust.org.uk/george-inn).

Opening hours: Mon-Wed 11am to 11pm, Thu 11am to 11.30pm, Fri-Sat 11am to midnight, Sun 11am to 10.30pm.

Cost: Free.

Transport: London Bridge tube/rail.

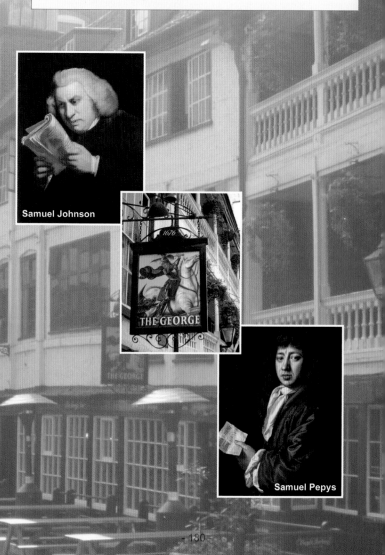

Samuel Johnson

Samuel Pepys

GEORGE INN

The George Inn is a popular pub near London Bridge on the south side of the Thames, dating from the late medieval period. It's Grade I listed and is tucked away in a cobbled courtyard just off Borough High Street. The George is one of London's only two surviving coaching inns and is the only one that's galleried. It's owned and leased to the current tenants by the National Trust.

The pub and its surrounds are steeped in history. The first map of Southwark (1543) shows it as the 'Gorge', and previously it was called the George and Dragon. Shakespeare was a visitor – the Globe Theatre was a short distance away – as was Charles Dickens; the pub is mentioned in *Little Dorrit*. Pepys and Johnson would also have drunk here. The George is located next to the White Hart, on a site where the inn was mentioned by Shakespeare in *Henry VI, Part 2* and by Dickens in *The Pickwick Papers*; its other neighbour is the site of the Tabard, an inn established in 1307, where (in 1388) Chaucer began work on *The Canterbury Tales*.

The George was rebuilt in 1676 after a fire which destroyed most of medieval Southwark. Later, the Great Northern Railway used it as a depot and pulled down two of its fronts to build a warehouse. As a result, just the south face remains. It's still a large inn, but much smaller than it was originally, when it was huge; only around a third survives.

Coaching inns were built around a courtyard so that coaches could enter and be unloaded in a sheltered, protected place. The ground floor would have been rooms for eating and drinking, with bedrooms above, entered by external galleries. In its heyday, the George would have received 70 or 80 coaches a week, and it was only one of Southwark's galleried inns, which were the bus and railway termini of their day. The City gates and London Bridge were locked at night, so there was a constant demand for accommodation from those arriving late.

The cosy, historic interior has an authentic atmosphere of yesteryear. The ground floor is divided into a series of bars. The Old Bar used to be a waiting room for coach passengers, while the Middle Bar was a coffee room (patronised by Dickens). The bedrooms were upstairs, in the galleried part of the building, which is now a restaurant. In summer, performances of Shakespeare's plays are staged in the inn yard.

Address: **83 Bermondsey St, SE1 3XF (020-7407 8664, fashiontextilemuseum.org).**

Opening hours: **Exhibition space and shop: Tue-Sat, 11am to 6pm. Closed Sun-Mon. See website for exhibition dates.**

Cost: **For changing exhibits, £11.50 adults, £10.50 concessions, £9.50 students, under-12s free. Free entrance to shop and café.**

Transport: **London Bridge tube/rail.**

FASHION & TEXTILE MUSEUM

Appropriately sited in the heart of trendy Bermondsey village, this is an exhibition centre for fashion and textile design. It was founded by one of Britain's most famous fashion designers, Zandra Rhodes, who was part of the new wave of designers who put London at the forefront of the international fashion scene in the '70s. She's also known for her distinctive personal appearance, including pink or red hair (she used to favour green), theatrical makeup, artistic jewellery and brightly coloured clothes.

Zandra Rhodes Enterprises is based a couple of doors down the road (at 81 Bermondsey Street), but the Fashion and Textile Museum has been taken over (and is now owned by) Newham College. It's housed in a striking building designed by the Mexican architect Ricardo Legorreta (who's noted for his use of bright colours, play of light and shadow, and solid geometric shapes), with an eye-catching orange and pink exterior, very much a splash of Mexican colour in the heart of London.

The website claims that it's 'a cutting edge centre for contemporary fashion, textiles and jewellery'. It has a small permanent collection – of designs by Zandra Rhodes – and changing exhibitions exploring elements of fashion, textiles and jewellery. There's also an Academy which runs courses and a café (called, helpfully, The Cafe@FTM), and the museum has an archive that can be visited by appointment. The small shop is a good place to buy interesting and unusual accessories and jewellery by up-and-coming designers. The museum holds a series of fashion-related events and talks – see website for details.

The FTM isn't quite on the London radar, partly due to the entrance fee and the lack of a significant permanent exhibition. However, it's a worthy addition to the capital's attractions and it's worth keeping an eye on the website to check forthcoming exhibitions. Like fashion itself, which by its nature is constantly changing, so are the exhibitions. Past ones include The Little Black Dress, The Evolution of Underwear, Sampling the '70s and Tommy Nutter: The Rebel on the Row, about the noted Savile Row tailor.

CINEMA MUSEUM

Tucked away in a lively part of south London, close to the Elephant and Castle, this is a must for cinema lovers. According to the website, it's 'devoted to keeping alive the spirit of cinema from the days before the multiplex' – a noble aim. The Cinema Museum is a charitable organisation founded in 1986 by Ronald Grant and Martin Humphries from their own private collection of cinema history and memorabilia. It's housed in the Victorian finery of the administration block of the former Lambeth Workhouse, where Charlie Chaplin lived for a time as a child (which seems highly appropriate from the museum's perspective).

Ronald Grant began collecting as a child and at the age of 15 began work as an apprentice projectionist with Aberdeen Picture Palaces Ltd., an associated company of James F. Donald Ltd. Later, he worked at the British Film Institute and at the Brixton Ritzy. A chance trip back to Aberdeen allowed him to salvage and save from destruction many items from the James F. Donald cinemas. This Aberdeen memorabilia is at the heart of the Cinema Museum's collection. As cinemas around the country began to close during the '60s and '70s, the collection grew.

The museum's unique collection of artefacts, equipment and memorabilia reflects the glory and history of cinema from the 1890s to the present. It's a comprehensive collection covering all aspects of the cinema, from the architecture and fittings of cinemas to the advertisements that promoted the films.

The collection contains over a million photographs, including cinemas and cinema-going; an extensive collection of artwork and posters; projectors from all eras; cinema staff uniforms; fixtures and fittings, including ashtrays, carpets, seating and signage; plans and artwork for cinema architecture and interiors; and over 17 million feet of film. The printed archive contains a large collection of campaign books, cinema sheet music, fan magazines, periodicals and trade magazines, and there's also a library of books about actors and film criticism.

As well as the extensive permanent collection, the Cinema Museum also plays host to a varied and interesting programme of talks, film screenings, exhibitions, sales, live events, etc., with occasional presentations by film industry historians and insiders. Some of these take place in the atmospheric 36-seat screening room, complete with old cinema seats and illuminated signage. See the website for details of forthcoming events.

Address: The Queen's Walk, SE1 7PB (0333-321 2001, thedungeons.com).

Opening hours: Mon-Fri 11am to 4pm, Sat-Sun 10am to 4pm.

Cost: Standard ticket £27, anytime entry £36. Tickets can be combined with visits to other London attractions.

Transport: Waterloo tube/rail or Westminster tube.

LONDON DUNGEON

The London Dungeon is a tourist attraction on the South Bank that recreates various gory and macabre historical events in a black comedy style, employing a mixture of live actors, special effects and rides. Opened in 1974 by Annabel Geddes, the Dungeon was originally a wax exhibition comprising themed tableaux under the Tooley Street arches, where early characters included Boudica, Mary Tudor and Thomas Becket, along with scenes from the Norman Conquest. From the late '80s to mid-'90s it evolved to feature elaborate animated walkthrough attractions such as the Great Fire of London and Jack the Ripper (see page 233). Now owned by Merlin Entertainments, the Dungeon was rebranded as an interactive horror attraction, less historically-accurate and based around gallows humour. In 2013, the Dungeon moved from Tooley Street to the vast underground vaults of County Hall on the South Bank (next to the London Eye).

The all new multi-million pound attraction brings to life 1,000 years of London's history with a unique mix of live actors performing in scarily funny shows, special effects, edge of your seat surprises and exciting thrill rides. Guests embark on a journey through a dramatic London landscape going back ten centuries, where they're guided through ghastly plague-ridden streets, witness Guy Fawkes' dramatic plot to blow up Parliament, travel back to Jack the Ripper's bleak Whitechapel and 'enjoy' a close shave from Sweeney Todd. The London Dungeon features some 20 interactive shows and two rides employing around 20 actors.

The shows – guests are encouraged to participate – are staged on theatrical sets with special effects and depict events such as the Black Death and the Great Fire of London, featuring characters such as 'The Torturer', 'The Plague Doctor', and 'The Judge'. The experience also includes the 'Drop Dead, Drop Ride', a free-fall ride staged as a public hanging outside Newgate Prison in 1783, and the 'Tyrant Boat Ride' where you join the 'traitors' who conspired with Anne Boleyn in 1536 on her final journey (in the dark) along the Thames to The Tower of London, where you'll meet your fate.

A 'Dungeon Lates' experience (adults only) is held once a month (see website for dates) during the evening and includes a visit to the Dungeon Tavern (two free drinks) where you steady your nerves before descending into the bowels of the dungeon. There are also educational visits for schools.

Address: Lambeth Palace Rd, SE1 7JU (020-7898 1200, archbishopofcanterbury.org/about/lambeth-palace/visit-lambeth-palace).

Opening hours: Visits by pre-arranged guided tour only. The gardens are open on certain occasions during the summer, both as part of the National Gardens Scheme and for the North Lambeth Parish Fete in June. The palace is also open during Open House London weekend (londonopenhouse.org).

Cost: See website for information.

Transport: Lambeth North tube.

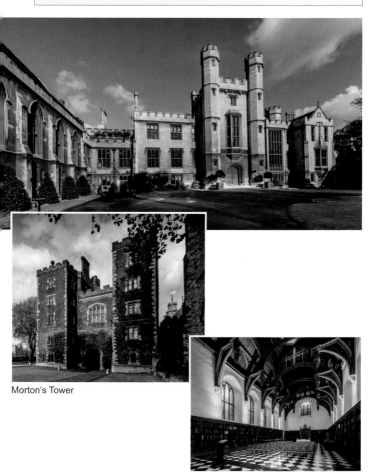

Morton's Tower

Great Hall

LAMBETH PALACE

You sometimes have to plan and work for your pleasures and that's the case here. Visits to the Palace are by pre-arranged guided tour, and you must be organised and patient to secure a place. They're very popular and there's been a waiting list for some years; see website for details, but expect to have to book up to a year in advance!

It's well worth it, because the Palace is arguably one of the capital's oldest and most overlooked treasures, partly, of course, due to the process involved to visit it. It's one of the most recognisable sights on the banks of the Thames and has been home to the Archbishops of Canterbury since 1200. The Palace is a short distance upstream from the Palace of Westminster, on the opposite bank, and was originally closer to the water, with the Archbishops coming and going by barge. (Some believe the name Lambeth comes from *loamhithe*, meaning 'muddy bank'.)

The Palace contains a number of London's few remaining Tudor buildings, some of them visible from the outside (which is some compensation for those unwilling or unable to wait for a year to secure a guided tour). There's an interesting mix of buildings from various ages, and the earliest part of the Palace dates from around 1220, the vaulted crypt, which is supported by Purbeck marble pillars. Sir Thomas More was interrogated here in 1534 by Thomas Cromwell and Anne Boleyn was forced to confess here by Archbishop Cranmer three days before she was executed in 1536. The attractive 14th-century Guard Room has displays of arms and some impressive portraits of old Archbishops.

The Early English Chapel dates from 1440, the early 15th-century Lollards Tower has a spiral staircase, and there's a fine Tudor brick gatehouse dating from 1495. However, many consider the Palace's jewel to be its 17th-century Great Hall (by Sir Christopher Wren) with its fine hammer beam roof.

Exhibits on display at the Palace include the gloves worn by Charles I on the scaffold and a Holbein-illustrated first edition of More's *Utopia*. The garden is the second-largest private garden in London (after Buckingham Palace), while in the front courtyard is Britain's oldest fig tree, planted in the 16th century.

GARDEN MUSEUM

Despite being described by the *Daily Telegraph* as 'one of London's best small museums', the Garden Museum (which used to be called the Museum of Garden History) is sometimes overlooked. Ironically, this is partly due to its great location, next to Lambeth Palace, on the bank of the Thames almost directly opposite the Houses of Parliament; it's ignored because people are concentrating on its famous neighbours.

The Garden Museum was founded in 1977 and over the past four decades a unique collection has been assembled through purchases, donations and bequests. Today the museum contains some 10,000 objects, each one of which in some way represents British gardens and gardening. It was deemed outdated and was cleverly redesigned in 2008, with an upper floor housing the permanent collection, which overlooks the events space in the church below.

It's the world's first museum dedicated to the history of gardening, and celebrates and explores British gardens and gardening through its collection, temporary exhibitions, events, symposia and garden. The permanent collection comprises three main categories: tools, ephemera (including prints, photographs and catalogues, giving an insight into the social as well as practical history of gardening) and a library.

The collection covers the subject in its broadest sense and demonstrates both the ingenuity and continuity of gardening over the centuries. Objects on display range from specialist equipment made for grand country estates to improvised tools created by enthusiasts in their own back gardens. The earliest objects on display include ceramics dating back several hundred years. The Victorian and Edwardian periods are particularly well represented, while there's also a good representation of gardening since 1950.

The museum is based in the deconsecrated church of St Mary-at-Lambeth, which dates from the 14th century (restored in 1850). It was chosen as a suitable site following the discovery in the graveyard of the graves of two 17th-century royal gardeners and plant hunters, John Tradescant (father and son – in fact, five members of the family are buried here). Elizabeth Boleyn (Anne Boleyn's mother) also rests here, as does William Bligh, captain of the *Bounty*.

In the churchyard is a lovely garden, which is a peaceful haven in central London. It's a recreated 17th-century knot garden, in a formal, geometric style with authentic period planting (seeds for which can be bought in the museum shop). There's also a highly-rated garden café serving delicious vegetarian food.

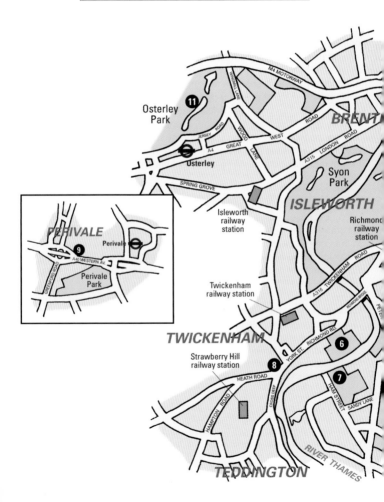

CHAPTER 6

WEST LONDON

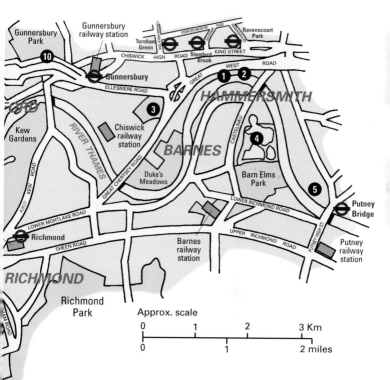

AT A GLANCE

Address: 7 Hammersmith Terrace, W6 9TS (020-8741 4104, emerywalker.org.uk/visit, info@emerywalker.org.uk).

Opening hours: Pre-booked tours (90 mins), Mar-Nov, Thu and Sat, can be booked via the website (see website for information).

Cost: Tours £15 per head.

Transport: Stamford Brook tube.

7 HAMMERSMITH TERRACE

This is one of Britain's most authentic Arts and Crafts interiors, the former home of printer and collector Emery Walker (1851-1933), later Sir Emery, friend and mentor to design guru William Morris (see **The Red House** on page 309 and **Kelmscott House** on page 197). It's one of a terrace of 17ft tall, narrow houses built in the 1750s between Chiswick Mall and Lower Mall (Hammersmith) on the north bank of the Thames, which became popular with artists and other creative types.

Emery Walker was a coachbuilder's son who found success by developing new printing techniques and whose move to Hammersmith brought him into close proximity with William Morris. Their shared socialist beliefs drew them together in the 1880s and printing cemented their friendship. Indeed, Walker gave Morris the idea for his famed Kelmscott Press, the last major project of Morris's life.

Emery Walker moved into 7 Hammersmith Terrace in 1903, but had already spent 25 years at number 3 and many of its contents were moved down the road. From the outside, it's a traditional Georgian house; within, the decor and furnishings have been preserved as they were in Walker's lifetime. The interior is similar to how the homes of many key figures in the Arts and Crafts movement would have been: William Morris furniture, textiles and wallpaper, plus Middle Eastern and North African ceramics and textiles. There's also furniture and glass by Philip Webb (the architect of The Red House – see page 309), ceramics by William de Morgan and furniture by Ernest Gimson.

When Philip Webb died, he left all his possessions to Emery Walker, and many of these are displayed in the house, including significant items of his own furniture, books and personal belongings; when William Morris died, his widow also gave Walker some of his furniture and possessions. As a result, this modestly-sized house has been dubbed 'an internationally important Arts and Crafts time warp'.

Walker was a founder or committee member of many of the key bodies that propagated the ideals of the Arts and Crafts movement, and throughout the house there's evidence of his friendship with many of the key artistic, literary and political figures of the late 19th and early 20th centuries. The pretty, walled garden – which leads down to a wall embanking the river – is laid out as it was in Walker's time.

Address: Upper Mall, Hammersmith, W6 9TA (Dove pub, 19 Upper Mall, 020-8748 9474, dovehammersmith.co.uk; Kelmscott House, 26 Upper Mall, 020-8741 3735, williammorrissociety.org/our-museum/visiting-us).

Opening hours: Kelmscott House is privately owned but the basement and coach house are open on certain days (see website for information). The Dove: Mon-Sat, noon to 11pm, Sun, noon to 10.30pm.

Cost: Free.

Transport: Ravenscourt Park tube.

UPPER MALL, DOVE PUB & KELMSCOTT HOUSE

Hammersmith's Upper Mall boasts some of London's prime Thameside homes and is one of the best places in the capital for a stroll along the river. It also has The Dove pub and Kelmscott House, one of William Morris's former homes (see also **The Red House** on page 309).

At number 18 is The Dove, an 18th-century pub with a lovely riverside terrace, a popular viewpoint from which to watch the annual Oxford and Cambridge Boat Race. It also has what's claimed to be the smallest bar in England. The Dove used to be a coffee house, but has long been a pub and is many people's idea of what the perfect pub should be like.

The pub has an interesting history. Charles II and Nell Gwyn apparently used to visit for assignations. In 1740, the poet James Thomson wrote *Rule Brittania* in an upstairs room here, while the composer Gustav Holst also used to work in a room at the pub. Today, it's intimate and cosy, which is fine if there aren't many other customers, but not so comfortable if there are. It does get very busy, which means that service can be slow, while the toilets aren't to everybody's taste.

At number 26 is the attractive Georgian building Kelmscott House, where William Morris lived from 1879 until his death in 1896. Built in around 1780 and originally called 'The Retreat', Morris renamed it after his home in Oxfordshire, Kelmscott Manor, and sometimes travelled between the two by boat (those were the days!). In 1891, Morris established the Kelmscott Press at number 16. Today, the William Morris Society occupies the basement of Kelmscott House, the entrance to which is down steps leading from the driveway.

There's a small, interesting museum, with a collection of Morris's drawings, some lovely furniture and his printing press. The photographs of Morris himself are especially revealing – he looks rather more approachable and lively than many of his Victorian contemporaries appear to have been. The coach house was used for meetings for socialist groups that William Morris was involved with, and the likes of Keir Hardie and George Bernard Shaw lectured here.

Address: Burlington Lane, W4 2RP (020-3141 3350, chgt.org.uk).

Opening hours: House: Apr-Oct, Sun-Wed and bank holidays, 10am to 5pm; Nov-Mar closed to visitors (although open in Mar for the Camelia Festival – see website). Conservatory: daily, 10am to 4pm. Gardens: daily, 7am to dusk. Café: daily from 8.30am (closing time varies). Confirm times with website.

Cost: Gardens: Free. House & Kitchen Garden: £11 adults, £5.50 concessions (jobseekers & students), £5.50 children (5-17), under 5s free, £23.50 families (two adults).

Transport: Turnham Green tube or Chiswick rail.

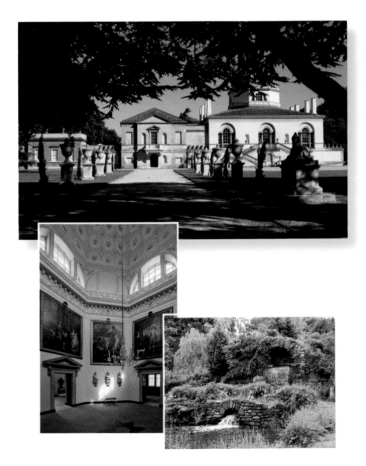

CHISWICK HOUSE & GARDENS

Nestled unexpectedly in affluent, mock-Tudor Chiswick suburbia is a glorious piece of Palladian Italy, with plenty of surrounding green space in which to walk, picnic, let off steam and become happily lost. Chiswick House was completed in 1729, the vision of the third Earl of Burlington, who'd been inspired by the architecture he saw during his 'grand tours' of Italy. It's one of England's finest examples of neo-Palladian design, i.e. modelled on the architecture of ancient Rome and 16th-century Italy.

It wasn't built as a private residence so much as a showcase for art and a venue for entertaining; the Earl played host to the luminaries of the day, including Alexander Pope and Handel. The design of the house echoes that of classical temples and is the result of a collaboration between the Earl and the architect William Kent.

There's much to see in the house, including eight beautiful landscape views of Chiswick by the 18th-century Dutch artist Pieter Andreas Rysbrack (they can also be seen on the website); The Chiswick Tables, which are some of the best examples of English neo-Palladian furniture; The Blue Velvet Room Ceiling, an ornate blue and gold representation of the goddess of architecture; statues of the architects Palladio and Inigo Jones; two porphyry urns; the Coffered Dome in the Upper Tribunal; carvings of the pagan god The Green Man in the fireplaces of the Green Velvet Room; beautiful, half-moon apses in the Gallery; a splendid lead sphinx and much more.

The gardens are also full of interest and are of historical significance: they were the birthplace of the English Landscape movement, i.e. a style of sweeping elegance which replaced the previous formality. They offer grand vistas and hidden pathways, dazzling flower displays and architectural treats. There's also a 19th-century conservatory (famous for its large collection of camellias, the largest in the western world and celebrated in a festival in Feb-Mar), a Classic Bridge, cricket pitch, lake, Italian garden, statues, walled gardens and much more. The gardens were recently restored (at a cost of £12m), in one of the largest and most ambitious garden regeneration projects ever undertaken in Britain.

The café, designed by Caruso St John, was named RIBA London Building of the Year in 2011; one of London's best park cafés, it serves delicious sandwiches, soups and the best of modern British cooking.

Address: Queen Elizabeth's Walk, SW13 9WT (020-8409 4400, wwt.org. uk/wetland-centres/london).

Opening hours: Daily except for 25th Dec. Winter (until the end of Mar), 9.30am to 4.30pm; summer, 9.30am to 6pm.

Cost: £13.40 adults, £11.36 concessions, £8.13 children (4-16), under 4s free, £36.63 families (2 adults and 2 children aged 4-16).

Transport: Barnes rail.

LONDON WETLAND CENTRE

Situated in the elegant, upmarket west London enclave of Barnes, this is slightly off the radar for many visitors to the capital, which is a pity because there's nothing quite like it in any other major city; an amazing and unexpectedly large wildlife habitat near the centre of the metropolis. Without wishing to oversell it, this must be one of London's wonders, despite being one of the least 'London-like' attractions. As *The Times* said of the Centre 'when you enter, you leave London behind'.

The London Wetland Centre extends to over 100 acres (42ha) on land formerly occupied by several small reservoirs, which were converted into a wide range of wetland features and habitats, including grassland, mudflats and reed beds. This incredibly rich wetland reserve is managed by the Wildfowl and Wetlands Trust (which runs a total of ten sites in the UK) and is recognised as a Site of Special Scientific Interest.

The Centre is probably Europe's best urban wildlife viewing area and is an important site, not just for birds (over 180 species, including many that aren't found elsewhere in London) but also for bats, other small mammals, insects and amphibians. It's a haven for hundreds of species, but there are a handful of 'stars' that many visitors are particularly excited to spot. In the summer months these include the gregarious lapwing and the undeniably cute water vole, while the winter months bring significant numbers of snipe, bittern and other migrating birds to the reserve.

The London Wetland Centre is a notably user-friendly environment, where you're loaned binoculars for your visit and small fishing nets are provided for children, with the facility to examine catches later. Free guided walks are organised with experts or you can just wander off on your own and stroll along the walkways among the lakes, pools, meadows and reed beds. The reserve also features a heated viewing observatory, a bat house, hides where you can get up close to the wildlife, and an adventure area and interactive discovery centre for children.

There's also a regular programme of children's activities at weekends and during holiday periods (see the website for details), and an impressive visitor centre, with a gift shop, café and a cinema showing a short documentary about wetlands.

We will leave the last words to the esteemed wildlife film-maker and television presenter Sir David Attenborough: 'The London Wetland Centre is the ideal model for how mankind and the natural world can live side by side in the 21st century'. Praise indeed!

AT A GLANCE

Address: Bishop's Ave, SW6 6EA (020-7736 3233, fulhampalace.org).

Opening hours: Palace: Wed-Sun 10.30am to 4pm. Walled garden: 10.15am to 3.45pm. Café: 9,30am to 4pm. Hours may be extended in summer (see website). Botanical gardens: daily, dawn to dusk. Regular history tours and garden walks are available on selected days (see website for dates and bookings).

Cost: Entrance to the palace and grounds is free. Tours £8.

Transport: **Putney Bridge tube or Putney rail.**

Walled Garden

Café

FULHAM PALACE

Fulham Palace is a well-kept local secret; an unexpected, tree-enclosed haven in west London, with lovely gardens in a tranquil, Thameside location. It's one of London's oldest and most historically significant buildings, yet strangely little known outside the local area.

The palace was the country home of the Bishops of London for over 900 years, and excavations in recent years revealed several former large-scale buildings and evidence of settlements dating back to Roman and Neolithic times. The land is recorded as belonging to the Bishop of London in 700AD, and the palace was their country house from at least the 11th century and their main residence from the 18th century until 1975. Today it's owned by the Church Commissioners and leased to Hammersmith and Fulham Council and the Fulham Palace Trust.

Much of the surviving palace building dates from 1495 and is Grade I listed. It encompasses a variety of different building styles and ages, while the extensive gardens (the grounds used to extend to over 30 acres, but only 12 remain) contain a range of international plant species, some dating from the 18th century. The gardens were famous and home to a number of the country's botanical firsts, although their fortunes vacillated as some bishops weren't interested in them. The palace used to have England's longest moat (infilled in 1924), which enjoyed direct access to the Thames.

The gardens are now an ideal picnic spot, with lawns, unusual tree species (including black American walnut, cork and Virginian oak) and an 18th-century walled herb garden with an orchard and a wisteria-draped pergola. There are also regular displays of sculpture and other art works in the gardens. Part of the palace grounds were converted into allotments during World War II, which have remained in use ever since allowing local people to grow their own vegetables, fruit and flowers. Although the palace has its own chapel, the gardens adjoin the churchyard of the neighbouring parish church, All Saints Church, where several former bishops are buried.

Fulham Palace also has a shop, a museum, a contemporary art gallery and a café, which overlooks the grounds. The museum collection includes paintings, archaeology and artefacts, as well as the palace itself, as demonstrated by the 1:50 scale model of the building. The collection is displayed in two palace rooms which have been restored to their original Georgian splendour. The palace is said to be haunted by the ghosts of Protestant heretics, who were persecuted in the Great Hall.

Address: Richmond Rd, TW1 2NL (020-8892 5115, english-heritage.org.uk/visit/places/marble-hill-house).

Opening hours: At the time of publication the house was closed for refurbishment (see the website for updates). Park: daily, 6.30am to 5.30pm year round. Café: open most days from 8am to 4pm.

Cost: Park free. House: see website for information. English Heritage members free.

Transport: Richmond tube/rail. The house can also be reached via a scenic walk along the Thames footpath.

MARBLE HILL HOUSE

Marble Hill House is a beautiful Palladian villa on the north bank of the Thames, the last complete survivor of the beautiful villas and gardens that bordered the Thames between Richmond and Hampton Court in the 18th century. It's little known – despite its proximity to the much-visited Hampton Court Palace – but fine enough to be included in the journalist Sir Simon Jenkins's book, *England's Thousand Best Houses*. The house is now owned by English Heritage.

It was built between 1724 and 1729 for Henrietta Howard, Countess of Suffolk, King George ll's mistress (built when he was still Prince of Wales), by the architect Roger Morris, who collaborated with Henry Herbert, Earl of Pembroke (one of the 'architect earls'). In 1723, the Prince had given the Countess £11,500 (around £1.7m today) to furnish her with a retreat from crowded, insalubrious 18th-century London. It was set in 66 acres of glorious riverside parkland, the Marble Hill Park.

The house was built to a compact design, with tightly controlled elevations, which became influential and a standard model for villas in southern England and much further afield, including plantation houses in the American colonies. Its grand interiors have been beautifully restored and conjure up the atmosphere of fashionable Georgian life better than almost anywhere else in Britain.

The Great Room has five architectural *capricci* by the Italian painter Giovanni Paolo Pannini and ornate gilded decoration, while the dining parlour has hand-painted Chinese wallpaper. The house also contains a collection of early Georgian furniture and some fine paintings, as well as the Lazenby Bequest Chinoiserie collection.

The gardens of Marble Hill House are linked to Ham House (see page 207) on the opposite southern bank of the river by Hammerton's Ferry (hammertonsferry.com), a pedestrian and cycle ferry service across the Thames. It's one of only a few remaining ferry routes in London that hasn't been replaced by a bridge or tunnel, operating at weekends and on weekdays from March to October (£1 adults, 50p children under 16, £1 adult bike, 50p child bike, buggies and dogs free).

AT A GLANCE

Address: Ham St, Ham, TW10 7RS (020-8940 1950, nationaltrust.org.uk/ham-house).

Opening hours: House: daily, Mar-Oct, noon to 4pm (see website for exact dates and opening times). Garden: usually 10am to 5pm. Shop & Café: 10.30am to 4pm.

Cost: Entry to the House and Garden: £6.50 adults, £3.25 child, £16.25 family. See website to confirm prices. National Trust members free.

Transport: Richmond tube/rail or Twickenham rail.

HAM HOUSE

Perhaps better known than its neighbours, Marble Hill House (see page 205) and Strawberry Hill, but still ignored by many, Ham House is an unusually complete 17th-century survivor on the Thames, rich in atmosphere and history. It's owned by the National Trust and is one of London's architectural and garden gems, but often overlooked, despite being only a short journey from central London. The name Ham comes from an old English word for 'a place in the bend in the river'.

Ham House was built in 1610 for Sir Thomas Vavasour, Knight Marshal to James I, and was extended and refurbished as a palatial villa under the ownership of Lord and Lady Dysart. It was mainly the vision of Lady Dysart, Elizabeth Murray, who's variously described as ambitious, beautiful, greedy and sharp-witted. She was also a renowned political schemer, involved with the restoration of the monarchy after the Civil War.

The Lady must also have been a fine time manager, as she and the Lord produced 11 children! Her hold on the house is said to continue to this day: her ghost and that of her dog still walk the corridors of what's reputed to be a very haunted property.

Ham House has rooms of sumptuous splendour, including walls hung with tapestries, rich fabrics and rococo mirrors. Meticulous restoration has created an atmosphere redolent of its original splendour. There are spectacular collections of furniture, textiles and paintings, while Ham has a notable collection of Coade Stone statues (Coade is a hard ceramic, which is cast and fired, named after its inventor Eleanor Coade); the statue 'River God' outside the front of the house is one of the largest pieces of Coade ever produced.

One of the most remarkable survivors at the house is the 17th-century formal garden. Most were replaced in the following two centuries by then-fashionable natural garden landscapes, but these have been little changed for over 300 years and include Britain's oldest orangery and a lovely, trellised cherry garden.

AT A GLANCE

Address: **268 Waldegrave Rd, TW1 4ST (020-8744 1241, strawberryhillhouse.org.uk).**

Opening hours: **House: Sun-Wed, 11am to 4pm. House closed Thu-Sat. Garden & Garden Café: Sun-Thu, 10am to 4pm. Confirm times with website. A range of tours can also be booked via the website.**

Cost: **£12.50 adults, £6.25 student, under 16s free. Tours: £20 adult, £15 student.**

Transport: **Strawberry Hill rail.**

Horace Walpole

STRAWBERRY HILL HOUSE

The Strawberry Hill website claims that visiting it is a 'truly theatrical experience', which is true in relation to this Gothic castle of undoubted charm and originality. Many claim that it's Britain's finest example of Georgian Gothic architecture and interior decoration.

Built in 1698, it was originally a modest house, but from 1747 was transformed by Horace Walpole (1717-1797), the son of Sir Robert, Britain's first Prime Minister. Horace was an art historian, antiquarian and man of letters, who wrote *The Castle of Otranto*, considered to be the first Gothic novel, while his collected *Letters* are of great social and political interest. He was also a dedicated collector, and Strawberry Hill was created to house his huge collection of 'treasures'. Much of the collection was sold in a great sale held in 1842.

Whereas nearby houses like Marble Hill (see page 205) were based on classical traditions, Walpole used the architecture of Gothic cathedrals as his inspiration. Between 1747 and 1797, he doubled Strawberry Hill's size, creating Gothic rooms and adding battlements and towers as he saw fit. The project developed and evolved in the way that medieval cathedrals did, over time and with no fixed overall design. Walpole added new features over a period of 30 years, to create something resembling a white wedding cake. Further additions were made after his death by Countess Waldegrave.

Walpole inspired a new fashion for Gothic, in both architecture and literature, and Strawberry Hill was something of a sensation in its day. He occasionally opened it to the public and the house was his lifetime hobby and joy. It's full of clever details, e.g. windows and shutters that slide into walls so as not to obstruct the view, which Walpole thought integral to a room.

By the end of the 20th century, the house had fallen into disrepair and it closed for restoration, the money coming from the Heritage Lottery Fund and World Monuments Fund, among others. It reopened in October 2010 after the first phase of an £8.9m restoration, involving the fabric of the house, including the conservation of the huge collection of painted renaissance glass. Later phases have seen contents added and the gardens remodelled, including the recreation of Walpole's striking and flamboyant Shell Bench.

Walpole intended a tour of Strawberry Hill to be a theatrical experience, and that it remains. You enter a gloomy hall and pass up a grey staircase before entering a splendid apartment, decked out in crimson and gold. Throughout the house there are features rich in detail and creative interest.

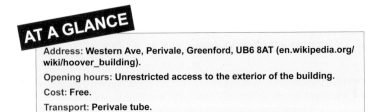

HOOVER BUILDING

A large, striking Art Deco pile, the Hoover Building was designed by Wallis, Gilbert and Partners and constructed between 1934 and 1938. It was built for the Hoover company and originally housed their main UK manufacturing facility for vacuum cleaners. At the time it was a potent symbol of the modern age, and now presents one of west London's largest, least-known visual treats, with great architectural impact.

During the Second World War, the factory manufactured electrical equipment for aircraft and tanks, operating 24 hours a day. The buildings were repainted and camouflaged with netting to avoid being spotted and bombed by German aircraft. After the war, a five-storey building was added and Hoover continued manufacturing here until the '80s, when production was moved to Scotland.

The building remained empty for some years, slowly falling into disrepair, and its future looked bleak until parts of it were Grade II listed. In 1989, Tesco purchased the Hoover Building and 16 of the 17 houses that backed onto the site. Plans were made to build a supermarket at the back of the site and restore the original building and canteen and convert them into offices. This was completed by 1992, with Tesco working closely with English Heritage during the design and construction. The supermarket mimics several design features from the original building, including its entrance, which resembles the fan window design of the Hoover Building's entrance. The supermarket is where the original production area was, while the Hoover Building to the front is effectively self-contained. The extensive Art Deco features of the exterior and common parts have been restored.

The Hoover Building was built from 'Snowcreate', a white concrete that stays looking new, whatever the weather throws at it. The building's glazed façade suggests a floorless expanse, but it has several floors. It's an American-style building, decorated with bright coloured faience (glazed ceramic inspired by ancient Egypt) and is floodlit at night, as it originally was, being part of the design scheme. It's lit with fluorescent green light and is visible from aircraft arriving at nearby Heathrow airport (the lights are now turned off at 10pm, following complaints from local residents).

Although dismissed by some architectural snobs as an unsubtle cake of a structure, most locals love the building, which has definite visual strength and appeal, notably when floodlit and viewed as a whole.

AT A GLANCE

Address: The name sometimes given to a stretch of the Great West Rd, which is to the north of Brentford and runs west from the western end of Chiswick.

Opening hours: Unrestricted access.

Cost: Free.

Transport: Gunnersbury tube/rail.

Pyrene building

Wallis House

Coty Cosmetics building

GOLDEN MILE, BRENTFORD

Brentford is west London's shabby corner, something of a poor relation when contrasted with its better favoured neighbours, including respectable Ealing and positively upmarket Chiswick and Kew. But don't let that put you off heading west to enjoy a number of unexpected architectural treats which date from the area's commercial past.

They lie along the Great West Road, which was opened in 1925. Several factories of architectural merit were quickly built here to take advantage of the good communications away from the centre of London and the availability of land for new building, some of it on a large scale. Many examples of these buildings' Art Deco architecture remain, including those described below (although more can be seen in the area).

Sadly, only the gates, railings and piers (in the Jazz Modern style) remain of the Firestone Tyre Company factory. But they're stylish and Grade II listed. The building frontage itself was rather scandalously demolished on a bank holiday in 1980, just before a preservation order was due to be served on the Art Deco architecture.

The Coty Cosmetics building was designed by Wallis, Gilbert and Partners, who were responsible for the design of many Art Deco buildings in the '20s and '30s, including the Hoover Factory (see page 211). Thankfully, the full frontage of this building remains. The Gillette Factory (designed by the splendidly-named Sir Banister Flight Fletcher, a sometime president of the Royal Institute of British Architects, RIBA) was built in 1936-7, but Gillette stopped using it in 2006.

The full frontage of the Pyrene fire extinguisher company building also remains (another Wallis, Gilbert and Partners design), while the frontage of the Currys' factory and head office (Grade II listed) has been restored by eminent architect Norman Foster's company (Foster and Partners for J. C. Decaux), which now occupies the building.

One of the Golden Mile's most striking buildings is Wallis House, which is yet another example of the work of Wallis, Gilbert and Partners. It was built between 1936 and 1942, originally for Simmons Accessories, who manufactured aircraft controls and similar, and was later occupied by Beecham Pharmaceuticals. It was redeveloped between 2005 and 2008 as flats, while retaining its basic fascia (Grade II listed), and is now part of a Barratt Homes Development.

Address: Jersey Rd, TW7 4RB (020-8232 5050, nationaltrust.org.uk/osterley-park-and-house).

Opening hours: House: usually Mar-Oct, Wed-Sun, 11am to 3.30pm. Park: daily, 9am to 5pm. Gardens: 10am to 5pm. Café & Shop: 10am to 5pm. See website for exact opening dates and times.

Cost: Park and grounds free. House & garden: £10 adult, £5 child, £25 family (2 adults). Garden only: £6 adult, £3 child, £15 family. Car park: £7. National Trust members free.

Transport: Osterley tube or Isleworth rail.

Entrance Hall (Robert Adam)

Sir Thomas Gresham

OSTERLEY PARK & HOUSE

Osterley House is a large, striking, National Trust-owned Tudor mansion set in gardens, park and farmland. It's one of London's last surviving country estates, once dubbed 'the palace of palaces'. The property is an original Tudor (1576) redbrick house of square design with four towers, built for Sir Thomas Gresham, an Elizabethan tycoon (who, among other things, was financial adviser to Queen Elizabeth I). It was not only somewhere for him to relax away from the city, but also a source of income. The land was fertile and well-watered, ideal for wheat, and he also established one of England's first paper mills here. Of the original 16th-century buildings, only the stable block survives.

The property was remodelled by the fashionable architect and designer Robert Adam for the (wealthy banking) Child family between 1760 and 1780. His vast entrance portico is particularly notable, an expression of classical refinement. The stunning interiors are one of the most complete surviving examples of Adam's work, with beautiful plasterwork, splendid carpets and fine furniture, all designed by Adam specifically for Osterley Park House. However, by the beginning of the 19th century, Osterley was no longer a main residence and, apart from a few brief periods of occupation, would never be again.

Today, the rooms are an ornate visual treat and you can explore the house with a handheld audio-visual guide, which helps to bring it to life. It remains much as it was in the mid-18th century, and the interesting 'below stairs' area allows you to imagine what it was like to be a servant here.

The house is set in 357 acres of gardens and parkland, one of west London's largest open spaces. However, it isn't the most tranquil, as the M4 motorway cuts across the middle of it and you can hear aircraft arriving and departing from nearby Heathrow airport. Nevertheless, there's some lovely planting, notably in the Pleasure Gardens (where the floral displays are at their best between June and September) and a fine collection of trees.

Beginning in the 1760s, the process of landscaping Osterley Park saw the ponds and streams integrated to form three long lakes – the Garden, Middle and North Lakes – which today are important wildfowl habitats. In the late 18th century the park's main attraction was its menagerie by the North Lake, which contained a host of rare and unusual birds. Substantial tree-planting over the centuries include the introduction of cedars and a collection of oak trees, which include an impressive cork oak, a Japanese Daimyo oak, Hungarian oaks and North American red oaks.

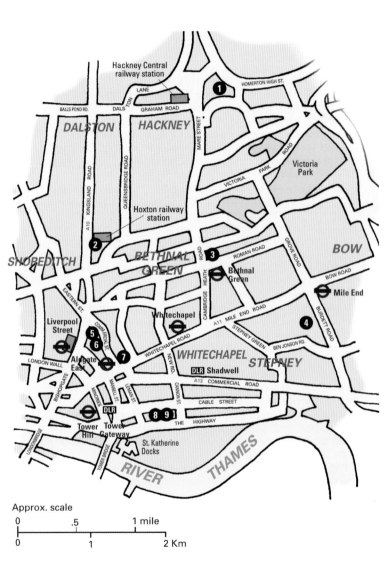

Approx. scale

0   .5   1 mile

0   1   2 Km

CHAPTER 7

EAST LONDON

Address: **2 & 4 Homerton High St, E9 6JQ (020-8986 2264, nationaltrust. org.uk/sutton-house-and-breakers-yard).**

Opening hours: **House & Garden, Feb to Dec guided tours on Wed, Fri & Sun. Closed Mon-Tue, Thu & Sat. Book via the website.**

Cost: **£8 adults, £4 children. Free for National Trust members.**

Transport: **Hackney Central rail.**

SUTTON HOUSE & BREAKER'S YARD

It's well worth making the effort to see this red brick Tudor mansion, which is stranded among housing estates in a poor part of Hackney. Built in 1535 by Sir Ralph Sadleir, Principal Secretary of State to Henry VIII, it retains much of the atmosphere of a Tudor home, despite alterations by later occupants. Highlights include original carved fireplaces, oak-panelled rooms (including a rare 'linen fold' room), Tudor windows and a charming, tranquil courtyard.

Sutton House is Grade II listed and owned by the National Trust, but its name is actually the result of an error. Thomas Sutton (who was allegedly the country's richest commoner) actually lived next door in a grand mansion that's now been demolished.

The house is the oldest domestic building in Hackney (and almost East London's oldest, just pipped by Bromley Hall, a much-altered but slightly older Tudor house, which is near the Blackwall Tunnel and not open to the public), dating from a time when the area was a country retreat from London. It was originally called 'Bryck Place', as it was the only brick building in a village of half-timbered properties. Brick at the time was expensive, and Sutton House is a rare example of a redbrick building from the Tudor period.

The house has been occupied by a variety of people: merchants, sea captains, Huguenot silk weavers, Victorian school teachers (it was a boy's and then a girl's school for a period) and Edwardian clergy. The façade was altered in the Georgian period (1714-1830), but it remains essentially a Tudor building. An exhibition tells the history of the house and its former occupants.

Sutton House fell on hard times in the second half of the 20th century, when hippies and squatters occupied it. Following their eviction, it was restored and renovated in the '90s. Amazingly, many of the original Tudor features survived this period – despite the building being used to host punk rock gigs for a while – and some of the hippy and squatter graffiti and murals have been retained, and provide an interesting contrast with the Tudor flavour of the rest of the house.

The building remains in use as a museum, which also has a café, art gallery and gift shop. There's an active schools education programme, together with other community programmes.

MUSEUM OF THE HOME

The Museum of the Home (formerly the Geffrye Museum) and its tranquil gardens are something of a haven in the busy, scruffy clutter of this part of Hackney, with its heavy traffic, Turkish shops and Vietnamese eateries. This isn't a part of the borough that's been gentrified, so it's ironic that the museum is devoted to the history of British middle class interior design, furniture, decorative arts, paintings and textiles, and traces the changing style of domestic interiors from the 1600s to the present day.

The original (Geffrye) museum was named after Sir Robert Geffrye (1613 to 1703), former Lord Mayor of London and Master of the Ironmongers' Company (a statue of Sir Robert is located at the back of the building). Under his bequest, 14 almshouses were built in 1715, primarily for the widows of ironmongers. These beautiful Grade I listed almshouses now house the museum, adding greatly to its appeal (visitors can explore the history of the building and the people who lived here, through tours, talks and displays). The Geffrye Museum closed in January 2018 for an £18 million re-development – increasing the space for exhibitions, events and collections by 80 per cent – and reopened in 2021 with a new name: Museum of the Home. The museum also has a new café and terrace.

The main exhibition is the Home Galleries 'rooms through time', which run the full length of the almshouse building, where you can explore contemporary and historic stories of home. Eleven period rooms are on display, from the Stuart era (1630) to the late 20th century, all displaying remarkable attention to detail. One of the aims of the museum is to provoke discussion and reflection about the ways we live (and lived), explore what home means, challenge assumptions and consider some of the issues facing society.

In addition there are regular exhibitions about subjects relating to the museum's displays, as well as events, seminars, workshops, performances and debates, while music and readings from the relevant period add to the atmosphere (see the website for the current programme of events). A new library – with beautiful high vaulted ceilings, overlooking the front gardens – is available for research and study, while on the ground floor there's an informal reading room.

The museum also has a number of period gardens 'Gardens Through Time', depicting garden design, layout and planting from the 17th to 20th centuries, and a walled herb garden containing over 170 types of herb. The gardens are designed to reflect the key features of middle class town gardens over the centuries. The gardens are open all year round and include a 21st-century, eco-friendly green roof, which highlight the challenges of gardening in a climate crisis.

Address: **Cambridge Heath Rd, E2 9PA (vam.ac.uk/info/young).**

Opening hours: **The new museum will open in 2023 (see website for updates) after a major re-development.**

Cost: **Free.**

Transport: **Bethnal Green tube.**

YOUNG V&A

The V&A Museum of Childhood in Bethnal Green closed in May 2020 and is being transformed at a cost of £13m into a new museum, Young V&A. It will be the UK's premier national museum designed by, and for, young people, from early years to teens – a place where they can learn, create and debate together, and design for tomorrow. It's intended to unlock their creativity and connect them with inspiring objects, projects and people from across the V&A's vast collection of art, design and performance. The new museum was originally due to re-open in 2022, but at the time of going to press in spring 2022 had been delayed until 2023. However, it should be well worth the wait.

The V&A cares for the nation's National Collection of Childhood, which comprises some 33,000 objects and 61 archival collections spanning 400 years, from 1600 to the present day. From the extraordinary to the everyday, from prototypes to mass-manufactured and hand-made objects, the collection includes one of Britain's oldest rocking horses, a sculptural installation of dolls' houses by artist Rachel Whiteread, and the archive collection of play leader and campaigner for children's right to play, Donnie Buck. The V&A also holds a range of archive collections relating to different aspects of childhood, including pieces from toy and children's clothing manufacturers, from individuals involved in the toy industry, and collections relating to schools and education.

The new museum will have three new galleries: Play, Imagine and Design. **Play** will include everything from the crowdfunded card game Exploding Kittens to chess, while **Imagine** will include exploring stories behind characters, such as Paddington Bear, Pikachu and the Loch Ness monster. **Design** will include an artist-in-residence programme entitled the Designer's House as well as displays that feature examples of contemporary design such as the micro-scooter. The galleries will showcase the vast scope of the V&A's collections – from 5,000 years ago to today – through interactive displays, dedicated workshops, and spaces for hands-on making. Young visitors will be invited to develop creative skills through performance, play and design, with an amphitheatre-style stage in Imagine, a free-play construction area in Play and a working Open Studio in Design.

There will also be a new Learning Centre which will enable the museum to become a leader in creative curriculum design to support teachers and educators nationally. Last but not least there will a licensed café, where stressed adults can calm their frazzled nerves.

Address: 46-50 Copperfield Rd, E3 4RR (020-8980 6405, raggedschoolmuseum.org.uk).

Opening hours: Wed-Thu, 10am to 5pm, and 2-5pm on the first Sunday of the month. School and group bookings Mon-Fri during term time. Confirm opening hours before visiting.

Cost: Free.

Transport: Mile End tube.

RAGGED SCHOOL MUSEUM

This is another little known London museum that doesn't immediately set the pulse racing, but it's a fascinating look at a sometimes ignored, poignant aspect of the capital's history. The Ragged School Museum is housed in a group of three canal-side warehouses, originally used to store goods transported along the Regent's Canal. Later it formed the largest 'ragged' or free school in London.

It was founded by Thomas Barnardo, who came to London in 1866 from his native Dublin to study medicine and then become a missionary in China. However, he was so shocked by the disease, overcrowding and poverty he found, and the lack of education for the poor, that he changed his plans and became a missionary in London's East End. The charity named after Barnardo (barnados.org.uk) is still active and is one of the UK's largest and most high profile.

In 1867, he opened his first 'ragged' school, where children could get a free basic education. A decade later, Barnardo's Copperfield Road school opened, and over the subsequent 31 years educated thousands of children. It closed in 1908, by which time more government schools had opened to serve the local area. (At their peak, there were over 140 ragged schools in London.)

In the '80s the buildings were saved from the threat of demolition, the Ragged School Museum Trust was established, with the museum opening in 1990. The idea was to tell the story of the ragged schools and the broader social history of the East End. At the heart of the museum is a recreation of a Victorian classroom, with authentic desks, slate writing boards, blackboards and even dunce hats!

Children can experience life in Victorian times (which is no bad thing, many would argue), with lessons led by a costumed actor. There's also a reconstruction of a domestic East End kitchen as it would have been in 1900. The schoolroom and kitchen are both hands-on, interactive displays, and paint a vivid picture of what certain aspects of life was like for the Victorian East End poor, a salutary lesson in these pampered times.

There are also several display galleries which tell the story of the surrounding area over the last 200 years, and special exhibitions are regularly staged, usually regarding subjects related to the district's cultural history.

Address: 18 Folgate St, E1 6BX (020-7247 4013, dennissevershouse. co.uk).

Opening hours: Thu 6-9.30pm, Fri 5-9pm, Sat noon to 9.30pm, Sun noon to 4pm. It isn't absolutely necessary to book a tour but highly advisable. Three tours are offered: Dennis Severs' Tour (limited to a small number of visitors at a time), Silent Night and Silent Visit. You can also arrange a private group visit (events@dennissevershouse. co.uk).

Cost: Dennis Severs' Tour £70, Silent Night £20, Silent Visit £15.

Transport: Liverpool St tube/rail.

DENNIS SEVERS' HOUSE

This is one of London's most singular, intriguing attractions, in one of its most magical settings. It's really a work of fantasy, designed to create an atmosphere redolent of the 18th century and paint a picture of what life was like then. It's the brainchild of an American artist, Dennis Severs (1948-1999), who purchased the house in the '70s when the old Huguenot district of Spitalfields was rundown and little valued. Today, parts of it have been gentrified and it's home to artistic luminaries such as Tracey Emin and Gilbert and George.

Severs began to live life in the house as he imagined its original inhabitants would have done in the 18th century, and he spent time in (and slept in) each room in order to 'harvest the atmosphere' of each one. As a result, he gradually gave life to an invented family, whose imagined lives became a detailed 'still life drama' for visitors to experience. They're a family of Huguenot silk weavers – the Jervis family – invisible and invented.

Severs filled the house with period fittings and furniture as well as authentic smells and sounds, to create a genuine atmosphere. Each of the house's ten rooms reflects a different era of the house's past, a snapshot of the life of the families who 'lived' here between 1724 and 1914. Dennis Severs died in 1999, but the house has been preserved and is open for tours, which last for around 45 minutes, including a short introduction.

You're 'instructed' to remain quiet and use your imagination during the tour, and it isn't recommended for children, all of which some people find a little bossy or precious on the part of those running the house. Others disagree and find this attitude healthy in our noisy era, when people seem incapable of keeping quiet or concentrating for more than 17 seconds.

The atmosphere of a bygone age is best maintained if you refrain from looking out of the windows – which allow the 21st century to intrude – and the night-time, candlelit tours are the most atmospheric.

Address: **Spitalfields Market, 105a Commercial St, E1 6BG (spitalfields. co.uk/public-art).**

Opening hours: **Unrestricted access to the public art, which is displayed in and around the area of the market. Traders Market, Mon-Fri & Sun, 10am to 6pm, Sat 11am to 5pm. There are also plenty of shops open seven days a week during normal trading hours.**

Cost: **Free.**

Transport: **Aldgate East tube and Liverpool St tube/rail.**

SPITALFIELDS PUBLIC ART PROGRAMME

Spitalfields is an old area of London, which takes its name from the hospital and priory, St Mary's Spittel, founded in 1197. The famous Spitalfields market began in a field next to the priory in the 13th century. In recent years the area has become something of a magnet for artists: Gilbert & George and Tracey Emin, among others, live and work in the area.

Perhaps inspired by this and as part of a drive to revamp and revitalise the area, the Spitalfields Public Art Programme was created to provide 'an exciting array of sculptures and soundscapes in and around Spitalfields Market'. Many of the works reflect the area's varied history and culture. Paul Cox's *Spirit* (from 2009), for example, which is in Bishop's Square, depicts six large, white, cartoon-like rabbits. It's a reference to the area's earliest days, when it was a grazing area for cattle next to the priory. Rabbits also live in large, close-knit communities, like the diverse communities of today's East End. Stella Vollner's *Cocoon Line* and *Tower Line* are made from woven structures and reflect Spitalfields' Huguenot silk weaving past. (Photographs of these, Paul Cox's work and other examples from the programme can be seen on the website.)

The artworks are constantly changing and being augmented by new works (see the website for information). Since 2020, Spitalfields has been home to the *Herd of Hope*, a 21-strong herd of life-size bronze elephants by Gillie & Marc, who are also responsible for *Together Forever on Wheels*, a bronze of Dogman and Rabbitwoman on vespas!

The inaugural Spitalfields Sculpture Prize was awarded in late 2010 to the splendidly-titled *Goat* – standing (11.5ft) on top of a pile of packing cases – by Scottish sculptor Kenny Hunter. It was apparently inspired by Spitalfields' 'rich, ongoing social history'. The goat is an image of persecution and sacrifice, while the crates are a nod to the market as well as to the area's long record of human movement, with its various waves of immigration (including Huguenot, Jewish, Irish, East European and Bangladeshi), and a reflection of change and travel.

The artworks add colour and interest to the area and to a visit to the market (the so-called Old Spitalfields Market, rather than the version that moved to Leyton in 1991, owing to traffic congestion in Spitalfields).

WHITECHAPEL GALLERY

Whitechapel is associated in many minds with grisly crimes rather than art – it was the setting for Jack the Ripper's murders (at least five and possibly more – see page 233) and the Kray Brothers' murder of George Cornell at The Blind Beggar pub on Whitechapel Road. But it's also the home of one of Britain's most forward-thinking and influential art galleries, which is sometimes under-appreciated and ignored by those outside the world of contemporary art, being sited away from London's hub of large, famous galleries in the West End.

The gallery is located on the north side of Whitechapel High Street in a striking building with a distinctive façade designed by Charles Harrison Townsend (who also designed the Horniman Museum – see page 295). Both museums are usually referred to as Art Nouveau or Arts and Crafts in style, although Townsend was an original architect and his style is difficult to pigeonhole.

Founded in 1901 to 'bring great art to the people of the East End of London', the Whitechapel Gallery exhibits the work of contemporary artists and is noted for its temporary exhibitions. It has a long-standing reputation for premiering the work of international artists, as well as supporting local causes and promoting artists who live and work in the East End.

It exhibited Picasso's painting *Guernica* in 1938 as part of a touring exhibition organised by the English artist and collector Roland Penrose to protest against the Spanish Civil War and, among many others, it hosted exhibitions that brought Pop Art to the general public and highlighted artists, designers and photographers who defined the 'Swinging Sixties'. The Whitechapel also premiered international painters such as Frida Kahlo, Jackson Pollock and Mark Rothko, and showcased British artists including Lucian Freud, Gilbert and George, David Hockney and Mark Wallinger. It has also exhibited art from Africa, India and Latin America.

In the later '60s and '70s the gallery became less significant and cutting-edge, as newer venues such as the Hayward Gallery at the Southbank Centre displaced it, but it bloomed again in the '80s under the directorship of the noted British art curator Nicholas Serota (he took the bold step of closing it for over a year for extensive refurbishment) and is well worth visiting regularly.

In addition to its exhibitions (see website for details), the recently expanded gallery offers historic archives, educational resources, art courses, a bookshop and a well-regarded café/bar (which alone makes a visit worthwhile).

Address: **12 Cable St, E1 8JG (020-3978 0820, jacktherippermuseum. com).**

Opening hours: **Daily, 10am to 5.30pm. Walks are also organised. Booking is via the website, although it isn't mandatory.**

Cost: **£10 adults, £8 children (also the fee for walks). A Virtual Tour is also available online for £10.**

Transport: **Tower Hill or Aldgate East tube.**

Battle of Cable St Mural

JACK THE RIPPER MUSEUM

Founded by Mark Palmer-Edgecumbe and opened in 2015, the Jack the Ripper Museum – controversially, it was originally intended to be a 'Museum of Women's History' – tells the story of the victims of the infamous Jack the Ripper serial killer in and around Whitechapel in the East End of London in the 1880s. The sobriquet 'Jack the Ripper' originated in the 'Dear Boss' letter written by someone claiming to be the murderer (widely believed to have been a hoax) that was disseminated in the media. The victims' (most of whom were prostitutes) throats were cut prior to abdominal mutilation – hence the 'Ripper' label – and at least three had internal organs removed, which led to the belief that their killer had anatomical or surgical knowledge. The killings shocked the world and spawned numerous theories, books and films attempting to solve the crimes, which to this day are unsolved and remain a mystery.

There were eleven brutal killings in Whitechapel between 1888 and 1891, five of whom – Mary Ann Nichols, Annie Chapman, Elizabeth Stride, Catherine Eddowes and Mary Jane Kelly (known as the 'canonical five') were murdered between 31st August and 9th November 1888. The investigation was unable to connect all the killings to the 'canonical five' murders, which were considered the most likely to be linked.

The museum – located in a historic Victorian house in Cable Street in the heart of Whitechapel – recreates the East London setting in which the murders took place and exhibits original artefacts from the period (such as the whistle used by police constable Edward Watkins to summon help when he discovered the body of Catherine Eddowes, and the truncheon and notebook case he was carrying), along with waxwork creations of crime scenes and sets. The five-room exhibition includes a recreation of the police station in Leman Street where detectives attempted to identify the murderer, the bedroom of victim Mary Jane Kelly and the scene of Catherine Eddowes' murder, with an effigy of PC Watkins standing over her, while in the basement is a morbid mortuary. The museum hosts a daily 'Jack the Ripper Museum Walk', following in the footsteps of the Ripper and visiting key sites associated with the murders.

Also worth a look nearby is the 'Battle of Cable Street' Mural (see opposite, battleofcablestreet.org.uk) at 236 Cable Street, which commemorates a violent clash between a march by Oswald Moseley's British Union of Fascists and anti-fascist demonstrators in 1936.

Address: 1 Graces Alley, E1 8JB (020-7702 2789, wiltons.org.uk).

Opening hours: Box office,11am to 6pm. Guided tours by appointment. A comprehensive programme of shows including cabaret, cinema, classical music, comedy, debates, lectures and theatrical productions is staged in the music hall (see website for details). The music hall's Mahogany Bar is open from 1pm on days with matinee performances and from 5.30pm for evening performances.

Cost: See website to book tickets or telephone.

Transport: Aldgate E or Tower Hill tube, Tower Gateway or Shadwell DLR.

WILTON'S MUSIC HALL

Wilton's dubs itself 'the oldest Grand Music Hall in the world'. It might also justly claim to add a new dimension to the term 'faded elegance', because that's what you find here, with this gloriously crumbling relic of a bygone age. It's one of the first generation of pub music halls that sprang up in London in the 1850s, most of which had disappeared just 50 years later.

The Mahogany Bar is older: it was built around 1725 and has always been a pub, trading under many names over the years, including 'The Albion Saloon' and 'The Prince of Denmark' in the 18th century. Back in the days when the British navy ruled the world, it was renowned in every major seaport in the world – to the extent that the revered public house near Wapping was said to have been better known on the waterfronts of San Francisco than St Paul's Cathedral. Its legendary status came about in 1828 when it was elaborately refurbished with a magnificent mahogany bar and fittings. This was unprecedented for a pub interior at the time and arguably established the look for the classic Victorian pub we know today. Sadly, the original fixtures and fittings have been removed over the years, but the atmosphere and sense of history remain.

The buildings that comprise Wilton's were originally five terraced houses. John Wilton opened the music hall in 1858, but it only remained open for 22 years, closing in 1880 when a successor was unable to renew the licence due to new fire regulations. A Methodist Mission took over the site and occupied it until 1956. Among other things, they allowed it to be used as a safe house during the 1936 Battle of Cable Street, and during the Second World War it provided shelter for people bombed out of their homes; thus the site became an important part of the community.

Subsequently, it became derelict and the years took their toll on the building and its fabric, although its crumbling state adds to its charm and atmosphere of shabby romance; 'sympathetic' repairs are made as funds become available. Wilton's is Grade II listed and one of the few surviving music halls in its original state, although it was only Sir John Betjeman's intervention in 1960 that saved it from demolition. Visit to marvel at its huge auditorium, with gleaming barley sugar twist pillars and an elaborate gilt balcony, all peeling paint and noble decay.

EASTBURY MANOR HOUSE

Eastbury Manor House is an impressive, brick-built Tudor property, architecturally significant and little altered since it was built in the 1570s. It's set in small, attractive gardens and is an important example of a medium-sized Elizabethan manor house, built on land that was once part of the demesne (manorial land) of Barking Abbey (founded in 666 and now in ruins, with one surviving gateway). It's Grade I listed and, although owned by the National Trust, is managed by the London Borough of Barking and Dagenham, and is used as an 'arts, heritage and community resource'. Weddings are also sometimes held here.

It was built to an H-shaped plan by Clement Sisley, a rich merchant, who bought the land following the dissolution of the Abbey by Henry VIII in 1539. He needed a lot of house space: he married three times and had 11 children. Eastbury was one of the area's first brick buildings – in Elizabethan times brick was rare, expensive and high status – and it also had glass windows and high chimneys, which also demonstrated its owner's wealth. The English Bond red-brick work on the exterior is enhanced with 'diaper-work' patterns in grey coloured brick.

Unfortunately, much of the original interior wood panelling was removed when the house was modernised, but it's being restored and the renovation has revealed some notable wall paintings. Those from the early 17th century show fishing scenes and a cityscape, and are a highlight of the Great Chamber. The house also has exposed timbers, a fine, original oak spiral staircase, lofty chimneys, a cobbled courtyard and a tranquil walled garden, all of which add to the Tudor atmosphere. Information panels tell the story of the house and its former inhabitants.

According to some commentators (although disputed by others), Eastbury Manor House played a notable role in British history, as the Gunpowder Plot of 1605 was allegedly hatched here. This was a failed assassination of James I, the plan being to blow up the House of Lords during the State Opening of Parliament. The house is also said to be haunted; apparently, renovation work on old houses tends to kick-start or increase paranormal activity.

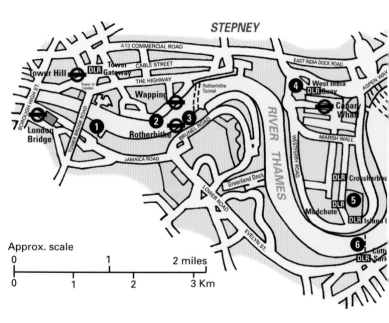

CHAPTER 8

EAST LONDON
– THAMESIDE

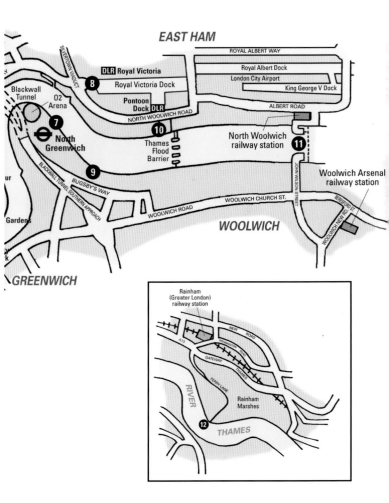

Address: **Shad Thames, Bermondsey, SE1 2NW (en.wikipedia.org/wiki/ shad_thames).**

Opening hours: **unrestricted access.**

Cost: **Free.**

Transport: **London Br tube/rail.**

SHAD THAMES

Shad Thames is a historic riverside cobbled street next to Tower Bridge in Bermondsey, southeast London, which is also an informal name for the surrounding area. The street, with Tower Bridge at its western end, runs along the south bank of the River Thames, set back behind a row of converted warehouses, before taking a 90° turn south along St Saviour's Dock (created in the middle ages by monks from nearby Bermondsey Abbey and named after their patron). The name Shad Thames is a corruption of 'St John-at-Thames', a reference to the Knights of St John, the former landowners. The local parish church of Horselydown – the medieval name for the area – was dedicated to St John when it was built in 1728.

In Victorian times Shad Thames was home to the largest warehouse complex in London – dubbeb the 'Larder of London' due to the vast quantities of tea, coffee, spices, dried fruit and other commodities stored there – which was completed in 1873 and consisted of an uninterrupted series of wharves, warehouses, mills and factories on both sides of the narrow and crowded roadway. During the 20th century the area went into decline, as congestion and containerisation forced shipping to unload goods further east, and the last warehouses closed in 1972. The area was redeveloped from the mid-1980s, when the disused warehouses were converted into flats, many with restaurants, bars, shops (etc.) on the ground floor.

Among the most striking features of atmospheric Shad Thames are the surviving wrought-iron gantries and walkways – now used as balconies by the adjoining flats – which criss-cross the street at various heights. Most now connect the Butlers Wharf building and the Cardamom Building, and were originally used as bridges to roll barrels and the like between the warehouses. The converted warehouses retain their original characteristic features, including brickwork, winches, large sign-writing, etc., most named after the commodities that were originally stored there, such as Cayenne Court and Tea Trade Wharf. (It's said that a century of spice storage had been infused into the brickwork and that the first residents could still detect its scent.) Various new buildings have been constructed, with similarly evocative names, such as Spice Quay Heights and China Wharf.

Today, Shad Thames is a wonderful evocative street, described by the art and architecture critic Nikolaus Pevsner as 'the most dramatic industrial street surviving in London', where imaginative new buildings provide a striking contrast with the grand Victorian warehouses.

MARINE POLICE

PRIMUS OMNIUM

FOUNDED 1798

FOR OVER 200 YEARS
POLICE HAVE PATROLLED
THE RIVER THAMES
FROM THIS SITE

STEPNEY HISTORICAL TRUST 1998

THAMES RIVER POLICE MUSEUM

This museum is located in the headquarters of the Metropolitan Police's Marine Support Unit, and provides a unique insight into the history of the world's first properly organised police force, which preceded the London police by 31 years. It's another of those obscure, hidden-treasure museums that London is famous for, and it's a proper 'old time' museum, nicely low-tech and full of nooks and crannies, which tells the story of a significant, often-ignored aspect of London's history.

The museum traces the history of the Thames River Police from its formation in 1798 to the present day. Based as it is in a working police station, visits are by prior arrangement, and visitors are conducted around the museum by the Honorary Curator, who's a serving police officer in the Marine Support Unit. It's of huge interest to anyone who's interested in the history of policing but also the history of the Thames; the river and its trade have played a significant role in the development of the British Empire and in London's rise to global economic and cultural importance.

The Thames Police was established as a result of the losses (calculated at the time to be at least £500,000 per year) suffered by importers – with a subsequent significant loss of import dues – while cargoes were unloaded on the unprotected Thames. Exports would also have suffered, although no estimates were made of the loss involved.

The first force had rowing galleys, each manned by a Surveyor (equivalent in rank to today's Inspector) and three waterman constables, all under the direction of a Superintending Surveyor. Ship and quay guards were also employed on a part-time basis. The initial force was around 50 officers, whose task was to police the 33,000 people who worked in the river trades (a third of whom were known criminals!). The force quickly justified itself, as the amount of money it saved in preventing thefts far outweighed the cost of setting it up and running it.

In 1800, the force's number increased to 88, thereafter to hundreds. By the late 19th century steam launches were being used (replacing the rowing galleys and sailing boats), and in the early 20th century paraffin-engined patrol boats were introduced. By 1910, most patrols were power driven, except for a few in the upper reaches of the river. In the early 21st century, other challenges face the force, notably terrorism – it's all documented here.

AT A GLANCE

Address: Rotherhithe St, SE16. St Mary's Church is at St Marychurch St, SE16 4NJ (stmaryrotherhithe.org) and the Mayflower at 117 Rotherhithe St, SE16 4NF (020-7237 4088, mayflowerpub.co.uk).

Opening hours: The Mayflower, Mon-Sat, noon 11pm; Sun noon to 10pm. See website for St Mary's service times.

Cost: Free.

Transport: Rotherhithe rail.

ROTHERHITHE STREET, MAYFLOWER PUB & ST MARY'S CHURCH

Rotherhithe Street is a notably complete 18th-century village, full of atmosphere and history, and only a few miles downstream from London Bridge. It's a long street of around two miles (London's second-longest after Oxford Street) that winds its way along the south bank of the Thames, following a large bend in the river. It used to have water on both sides – the Thames and the Surrey Docks – but the latter are now mostly filled in, although some bridges still survive. London's first enclosed wet dock was built at Rotherhithe in 1699.

A number of elegant 18th-century houses and 19th-century warehouses remain, mostly restored. Rotherhithe used to have a reputation for some of London's worst slums, and Dickens said that 'the very air would seem to be tainted'. Indeed, there are still some damp, dark lanes leading to the river that give a flavour of what it used to be like. Jonathan Swift decreed that Lemuel Gulliver (of *Gulliver's Travels* fame) was born in Rotherhithe.

Central to the area is St Mary's (aka St Mary the Virgin) Church, built in 1716 (although there's been a church on the site for at least 1,000 years and there's evidence of an earlier Roman building), and was one of the few churches in London to escape bomb or fire damage in the Second World War. It's an attractive building in yellow/white and red brick, sitting among old trees. By the south gate of the churchyard is a beautiful, narrow, three-storey house built in the 1690s.

Another local historic site is The Mayflower, a pub named after the Founding Fathers' ship that set sail from the pub's wharf in 1620 for the New World (calling at Plymouth on the way). Back then the pub was called The Shippe, and dates from 1550-60. It became the Spread Eagle and Crown in the 18th century, after having been rebuilt, and only became The Mayflower in 1957.

Captain Christopher Jones, the Mayflower's locally-born commander, brought the ship back in 1621, and its timbers were subsequently used in rebuilding the pub (which is, therefore, literally part of history) after the ship was left to rot in the river next to the pub. Captain Jones is also close by: he was buried in St Mary's churchyard in 1622, just a year after returning from the New World (which obviously didn't agree with him).

Today, the Mayflower is a small pub with a wooden terrace overlooking the river, enjoying fine views. It's one of the few pubs licensed to sell stamps, both British and American, the latter in view of its historic links with what is now the US.

MUSEUM OF LONDON DOCKLANDS

Sitting on the Isle of Dogs (a former island in East London, now bounded on three sides – east, south and west – by one of the largest meanders in the River Thames), this used to be called the Museum in Docklands. This is appropriate, as the museum is housed in a Grade I listed Georgian 'low' sugar warehouse, built in 1802; the Isle of Dogs was at the heart of London's docks, being the site of the West India Docks, East India Docks and Millwall Dock.

The three dock systems were unified in 1909 when the Port of London Authority took control of them. (With the docks stretching from east to west, and with locks at either end, the Isle of Dogs was once again almost a genuine island). The heart of the Museum of London Docklands collection is the museum and archives of the Port of London Authority.

The museum covers the period from the first port of London in Roan times to the closure of the docks in the '70s, and the area's subsequent redevelopment as a residential and financial area. It shows how the Thames became an international gateway, bringing invaders, merchants and immigrants to one of the world's longest-serving ports. The Museum of London Docklands is the best place in the city to get a sense of how crucial the Thames has been to the growth and rise to power of London. It explores the social and economic significance of the port of London, which for a time was the world's busiest. And it doesn't pull its punches by avoiding difficult subjects, for example London's part in the transatlantic slave trade; there's a permanent exhibition called London, Sugar and Slavery.

It's a large museum, with 12 galleries, including a children's gallery, and is modern and contemporary in its approach, using all the latest presentation techniques, including videos presented by Tony Robinson (a former comedy actor and the slightly excitable host of a long-running archaeological television programme on Channel 4, *Time Team*). There are lots of historical objects, models and pictures, with impressive displays and exhibits, including a walk-through of a working quay and a local back alley.

The museum also regularly hosts talks, temporary exhibitions and events related to the river and the docks. There's also a shop and restaurant. Somewhat overshadowed by its better-known big brother, the Museum of London (one of the world's largest urban history museums), the exhibit in Docklands is well worth visiting.

Address: Pier St, Isle of Dogs, E14 3HP (020-7515 5901, mudchute.org).

Opening hours: Park: dawn to dusk. Farm: Daily, 9am to 5pm. Café: Tue-Fri, 10am to 4pm, Sat-Sun, 10am to 5pm.

Cost: Free, but you're invited to make a donation.

Transport: Crossharbour, Mudchute or Island Gardens DLR.

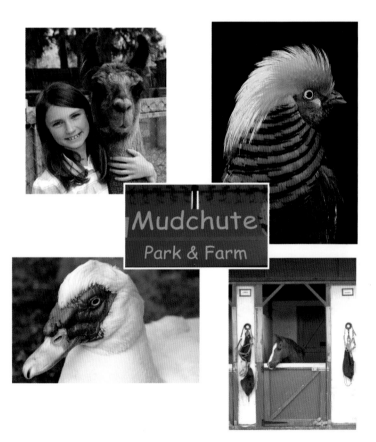

MUDCHUTE PARK & FARM

Mudchute Park and Farm is a slice of country life in the heart of East London, not only is it London's largest city farm (extending to 32 acres) but it's one of Europe's largest inner city farms, with over 200 animals and fowl. It sits just to the south of Canary Wharf, whose towers form an impressive, contrasting backdrop. Most people don't know it exists, which is perhaps understandable, as it's incongruous to find a working farm in the shadow of one of the capital's financial hubs.

Mudchute is an area of the Isle of Dogs, its inelegant name deriving from the fact that it was the site of the dumping of spoil from the Millwall Dock excavations. Silt from the channels and waterways was deposited here using a conveyor system, which sounds unfortunate but actually created an area of fertile, hilly land.

In 1974 the site was earmarked for the building of a high rise estate, having remained an untouched natural wilderness of flora and fauna for decades. However, there was a backlash from locals which led to the formation of the Mudchute Association in 1977 to preserve and develop the area. Farm animals and horses were introduced and plants and trees were planted.

The farm now has an impressive range of animals of various breeds, including cows (the Irish Moiled, a hornless breed), pigs (Gloucestershire Old Spot and Tamworth), sheep (Oxford Down and White Faced Woodland), goats (Anglo-Nubian and Pygmy), donkeys and llamas, while there are also small animals in Pets Corner such as ferrets, giant rabbits and guinea pigs.

Aviary birds include budgies, canaries, Chinese painted quail, diamond doves, golden pheasant, Java sparrows and zebra finches, while chicken breeds include Brahma, Light Sussex, Rhode Island Red and White-crested Black Polish. There's also a variety of ducks (including Call, Indian Runner and Muscovy), geese (Chinese and Greylag) and turkeys (Pied), plus an Equestrian Centre with some 25 horses and ponies.

The farm is an idyllic, verdant spot close to the centre of London, which allows visitors to relax and reconnect with nature. It's a genuine piece of countryside in a heavily urban environment and offers free access to a wide variety of animals and birds, while also providing a realistic impression of a working farm.

GREENWICH FOOT TUNNEL

A tunnel doesn't sound like a promising place in which to spend your valuable leisure time, but this is undoubtedly one of London's great Victorian engineering feats, with its own atmosphere and stark majesty. It's a pedestrian tunnel under the Thames in East London, linking Greenwich in the south with the Isle of Dogs to the north.

Designed by civil engineer Sir Alexander Binnie (who was also responsible for the Blackwall Tunnel and Vauxhall Bridge) for London County Council, it was built between 1899 and 1902 and replaced a ferry service that had been operating since 1676. The ferry service had become expensive and unreliable, and the tunnel was intended to allow workers living to the south of the Thames to get to work in the London docks and shipyards on or near the Isle of Dogs.

The entrance shafts at both ends sit beneath glazed domes, with lifts and spiral staircases allowing pedestrians to reach the sloping, tiled tunnel at the bottom; there are around 100 steps at each end. The tunnel is made of cast iron and is 1,217ft long and 50ft deep. The internal diameter is 9ft and its cast iron rings are lined with concrete, faced with 200,000 glazed, off-white tiles. The tunnel dips down in the middle. Its northern end was damaged by bombing during the Second World War, and repairs included a thick inner lining that considerably reduces the diameter for a short distance.

The tunnel's south entrance is near the restored ship, Cutty Sark. The north entrance is at Island Gardens, a park on the southern tip of the Isle of Dogs, which is well worth visiting for its superb views across the river to Greenwich, some of London's best and most iconic.

Some people think the tunnel claustrophobic, others spooky or atmospheric. Due to its depth, it remains cool, even on the hottest days. The acoustics, colour and style are certainly singular – with hints of public convenience, according to some – and the tunnel is definitely atmospheric and echoey, which can make it daunting at night, as can the thought of all that water above your head. The tunnel is part of the UK's National Cycle Route 1 linking Dover and Inverness, although cyclists must dismount and push their bikes through.

Address: **Drawdock Road/Millennium Way, Greenwich Peninsula, SE10 0BB (elliottwood.co.uk/projects/quantum-cloud-london and richardwilsonsculptor.com/sculpture/slice-of-reality-2000.html).**

Opening hours: **Unrestricted access.**

Cost: **Free.**

Transport: **North Greenwich tube. The sculptures can be seen on a stroll along the Thames Path.**

Quantum Cloud

Slice of Reality

THAMESIDE SCULPTURES

Although seen by many people as a money-guzzling political conceit, the Millennium Dome has certainly had beneficial effects on the surrounding area. Some of the vast sums spent on the project were channelled towards commissioning municipal art for its environs, and the Dome's new incarnation as the O2 Arena music and entertainment venue (the world's busiest and most successful) has also brought visitors and focus to the area. (The Millennium Dome itself, it should be said, is a striking piece of design and well worth visiting).

Quantum Cloud is a work by the English sculptor Anthony Gormley (best known for his work *Angel of the North* – see also **The Bellenden Renewal Area** on page 291), commissioned to sit next to the Millennium Dome and completed in 1999, ahead of the Dome's opening. It's 98 feet high – Gormley's tallest sculpture to date and, at the time of its construction, the UK's tallest sculpture – 52 feet wide and 33 feet deep, and is constructed from a collection of tetrahedral units made from 5-foot long sections of steel. Around 3.5 miles of steel section were used, weighing almost 50 tons.

These sections were combined using a computer programme with a random walk algorithm, starting from points across the surface of an oversized figure based on Anthony Gormley's body (generated by laser scans), which forms a hazy outline in the middle of the sculpture (not, at first, apparent). The sculpture has a great sense of movement and is splendidly sited with the Thames as a backdrop. The outer edges of its cloud structure also seem to resemble seabirds swooping over the river.

Quantum Cloud is located next to the river, but a second 'sculpture' (art installation is more accurate) is actually in it: *Slice of Reality* by the sculptor, installation artist and musician Richard Wilson is on the riverbed, albeit next to a stretch of the shore lined with benches, convenient vantage points from which to ponder it. *Slice of Reality* comprises a 20m-high cross-section of an ocean-going sea dredger.

It represents around 15 per cent of the original ship, sliced from the rest and mounted on the riverbed, seemingly rather precariously. It's the middle chunk of the ship, housing its habitable sections: accommodation, bridge, engine room and poop. As it weathers (indeed, in part, rots), it changes and becomes ever more interesting. It's supposed to continue the line of the Greenwich Meridian, as if the line itself had cut through the ship, and is designed to be an eerie reminder and celebration of London's long association with the sea.

AT A GLANCE

Address: **Tidal Basin Rd, E16 1AD (020-7511 5086, en.wikipedia.org/wiki/royal_victoria_dock_bridge).**

Opening hours: **Unrestricted access.**

Cost: **Free.**

Transport: **Royal Victoria DLR.**

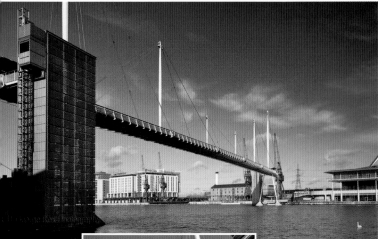

ROYAL VICTORIA DOCK BRIDGE

The Royal Victoria Dock was the largest of the three docks in East London's Royal Docks. It opened in 1855 on a previously uninhabited area of the Plaistow Marshes and was the first of the Royal Docks and the first London dock to be designed specifically to accommodate large steam ships. It closed to commercial traffic (along with the other Royal Docks) in 1980 and is now part of the redeveloped Docklands.

Today, one of its most striking sights is the high-level footbridge crossing the dock, linking Eastern Quay and Britannia Village to the ExCel Exhibition Centre and Custom House station, which are north of the dock. The bridge was completed in 1998 at a cost of around £5m, and was designed by the award-winning architects and designers Lifschutz Davidson Sandilands. It was designed so as not to impede shipping passing below, to afford protection against the weather, and to offer minimum resistance to the wind that tends to gust quite strongly on or near the river.

Some technical stuff: the bridge is in the form of an inverted, cable-stayed Fink truss, which is a style of bridge devised by the German Albert Fink in the 1860s. It has six masts rising above the deck, varying in height from 100ft at each end to 35ft for the smallest masts.

As part of the Docklands renaissance in recent years, the Royal Victoria Dock was designated a centre for sailing and rowing, and the bridge's shape is designed to reflect the masts of the sailing ships that use it. (As part of this 'sailing ethos', the nearby ExCel Exhibition Centre hosts the annual London Boat Show.) The bridge is made of steel and has a span of 418ft with a clearance above the water of 50ft, so that large yachts can pass beneath it.

The bridge is accessed at each end by a lift and stair towers – there's been talk of adding a glass passenger cabin or gondola travelling on a rail to the underside of the bridge to make it a transporter bridge. The bridge is a valuable addition to the area, not just as a means of crossing the dock, but as an elegant example of modern engineering – a large-scale piece of practical sculpture, according to some. It's also a great vantage point from which to enjoy sweeping views along the river and of the O2 Arena (Millennium Dome), the Docklands development and London City Airport.

Address: Thames Path, John Harrison Way, SE10 0QZ (01302-388 883, tcv.org.uk/greenwichpeninsula).

Opening hours: Wed-Sun, 10am to 5pm or dusk, whichever comes first. Closed Mon-Tue.

Cost: Free.

Transport: North Greenwich tube.

GREENWICH PENINSULA ECOLOGY PARK

As well as being a peaceful green haven near the heart of London, this natural area is a prime example of land being returned to its original form and function. Greenwich Peninsula used to be known as Greenwich Marsh, and consisted of marshes and agricultural land, including a large millpond; from the late 1880s it became heavily industrialised, with gas and chemical works and a large shipbuilding yard. The Blackwall Tunnel (which carries road traffic under the Thames), built in 1897, eradicated much of what was left of the area's fields and marshland.

From the '70s, the area's industries went into decline and the marsh began to reassert itself as land was left untended and became derelict. English Partnerships purchased the area in 1997 and began a huge regeneration project which included bringing 299 acres of neglected land back to life, restoring parts of the riverbank and creating the Greenwich Peninsula Ecology Park as a freshwater habitat.

The 4-acre park is something of a hidden gem, only around 15 minutes from North Greenwich tube and a similar distance from the iconic Millennium Dome, yet many locals are unaware of its existence, let alone visit it. This is a pity as it offers marshland, lakes, streams, wetland, woodland and a meadow; a wide variety of habitats in which to delight and relax. It also presents a rare opportunity in such a central location to have a close look at the banks of the Thames.

The Ecology Park consists of an inner and outer lake. The outer lake is continually accessible, the inner lake only through the gatehouse during allotted opening times. Wildlife thrives in the park, notably amphibians, birds and insects. Hides allow you to watch without disturbing them, and as the seasons change so does the wildlife and the extensive displays of flowers and plants – spring and summer are particularly colourful.

The park also offers a series of organised activities, including evening bat walks, lessons on nestbox building and coppicing, and summer family fun days. Schools can book visits to the park with the Trust for Urban Ecology, and you can volunteer to get involved with the trust and help maintain the park (see the website for details).

Address: **North Woolwich Rd, Silvertown, E16 2HP (020-7476 3741, london.gov.uk/what-we-do/environment/parks-green-spaces-and-biodiversity/parks-and-green-spaces/thames-barrier-park).**

Opening hours: **Daily, 7am to dusk.**

Cost: **Free.**

Transport: **Pontoon Dock DLR.**

THAMES BARRIER PARK

On the north bank of the Thames, with stunning views of the majestic Thames Barrier, lies one of London's newest and best-sited parks. It's the first riverside park to be created in London for over half a century and is quite a transformation for a site that used to be contaminated, having once housed petrochemical, dye and acid works and an armaments factory. Surface oils and tars had first to be removed from the site and contaminated water pumped from the underground water table.

Today, the Thames Barrier Park comprises 22 acres of lawns, trees (over 500), contoured, undulating hedges of yew and maygreen, fountains, wildflower meadows, a children's play area and sports facilities. There's a green trench running through the park, providing a sheltered microclimate for a 'rainbow garden' (strips of coloured plants). One of its most notable features is The Green Dock, selected colourful flowers and shrubs chosen to reflect the river's changing range of colours, moods, shades and shapes.

The park was designed by landscape architect Allain Provost of Groupe Signes and architects Patel Taylor, and opened in 2000. It's London's first post-modern park design, which gives it a fresh, new look, and it has won design awards in the UK and US thanks to its modern take on landscape garden design and adventurous planting.

Set between two modern housing developments, the Thames Barrier Park has quickly become an important open space and urban oasis in a part of London that seems mainly devoted to soulless, new-build shoebox flats (there's high security fencing between the park and the nearby residential developments). It's also a great picnic spot and an ideal vantage point from which to observe the Thames Barrier, one of the world's largest movable flood barriers.

The Barrier spans 520m across the river and protects central London from flooding caused by tidal surges (although some experts think it will be obsolete by 2030 and that a larger barrier will be necessary). Its ten movable gates are attractively sculptural, like vast metallic sails or shells (or even shiny armadillos according to some), and are particularly elegant in strong sunshine (something of a rarity in the British climate) or at dusk, when the Barrier is floodlit. It forms an ideal modern backdrop to this most modern of London parks, some of whose planting mirrors the barrier's shape and structure.

Address: New Ferry Approach, Woolwich, SE18 6DX and Pier Rd, E16 2JJ (020-8853 9400, royalgreenwich.gov.uk/info/200260/public_transport/61/ferry_services).

Opening hours: Mon-Sat and public holidays, 7am to 7pm, Sun 11.30am to 7.30pm. There are slight variations in times depending on whether you're travelling north or south (see website for exact times). No service 25-26th Dec and 1st Jan.

Cost: Free.

Transport: Woolwich Arsenal or North Woolwich rail.

WOOLWICH FREE FERRY

The Woolwich Free Ferry is a boat service across the Thames, linking Woolwich on the south bank with North Woolwich on the north bank. It also links London's orbital road routes, the North Circular and South Circular. The service is free and is operated by the Serco Group under licence from Transport for London.

There's been a ferry service across the river at Woolwich since at least the 14th century. The earliest reference to it is in a state paper of 1308, when the waterman who ran it, William de Wicton, sold his business and house to William atte Halle, for £10. In 1320 the ferry was sold again for 100 silver marks. The free ferry service wasn't introduced until much later, at the instigation of Sir Joseph Bazalgette, a civil engineer famous for developing the sewer network for central London and also for instigating the much-needed process of cleaning up the River Thames. The free ferry officially began operation on 23rd March 1889.

The 'fleet' currently consists of three vessels, which carry lorries and other road traffic, plus foot passengers. A vessel's licensed capacity is 500 passengers and 200 tons of vehicles. There's a maximum vehicle height limit of 15.5ft and a maximum width of 11.5ft.

The service carries over 1m vehicles and 2.5m passengers annually (occupants of vehicles are counted as passengers). Vehicle use of the Woolwich Ferry is still high, but foot passenger numbers have dropped considerably in recent years. This is a pity as it's an interesting, if brief (around 400 yards, so be quick with your camera if you wish to take photos) trip across a little-visited section of one of the world's great rivers.

It's quite common (especially during rush hours) for vehicles to have to queue beyond the next ferry departure, therefore it's advisable to avoid peak hours. The service is occasionally suspended due to inclement weather, most notably fog.

For foot passengers, bus services converge on both terminals; on the north side there's a small bus station, but many cross-river foot passengers take the foot tunnel (see this chapter) beneath the river, running alongside the ferry route. Further competition arrived in 2009 with the extension of the Docklands Light Railway to Woolwich, which runs under the river to the east of the ferry route. A planned bridge (the Thames Gateway Bridge) close to the ferry crossing would have spelled the end for the ferry service, but the project was cancelled in 2008.

Address: In the Thames on the north side of the river, at Coldharbour Point, off the Havering riverside path at Rainham in the northeast London borough of Havering (en.wikipedia.org/wiki/the_diver).

Opening hours: Unrestricted access.

Cost: Free.

Transport: Rainham (Essex) rail, which is so named to distinguish it from Rainham rail in Kent (don't go there!). Then walk or take a taxi to the Ferry Lane Industrial Area or Coldharbour Lane (there's a car park near the Tilda rice warehouse).

DIVER SCULPTURE

The sculpture's full name is The Diver: Regeneration and it's of an old-fashioned deep sea diver emerging from the river. It was installed in 2000 (at 3.30am in order to avoid river traffic) and was conceived as part of the London borough of Havering's regeneration of the river and the building of a riverside footpath at Rainham. It's said to be the only sculpture standing in the river Thames, although some people might point to Slice of Reality as another (see **Thameside Sculptures** on page 253).

It's the work of self-taught sculptor John Kaufman (1941-2002), who worked at a variety of jobs, while harbouring ambitions to be a sculptor. He was so keen on the project that he initially financed it himself, before finding sponsorship. It was a five-year labour of love, from drawing board to installation.

he sculpture was inspired by stories told by Kaufman's grandfather, who worked as a diver in the London Docks at the end of the 19th and early 20th centuries. The fingers of the sculpture's left hand are bent in acknowledgement of Kaufman's grandfather, whose arthritis was caused by the cold, unpleasant and dangerous conditions that divers had to endure.

The Diver was made from 300m of galvanised steel banding on a steel frame, plus around 3,000 nuts and bolts. It's 15 feet tall, 6 feet wide, weighs three tons and is thought to be robust enough to last for around a century, even in its corrosive salt water and mud environment.

It's little known outside the immediate area, which is a pity, as it's visually arresting and adds interest and a touch of humanity to this industrial stretch of the river. And it bears repeat visits: seeing it in different seasons and light conditions and at various tides provides different impressions. It's partly submerged at high tide, fully displayed at low tide, and totally submerged by spring and neap tides. There are a number of interesting photographs of the sculpture on the website showing its construction, installation and in situ.

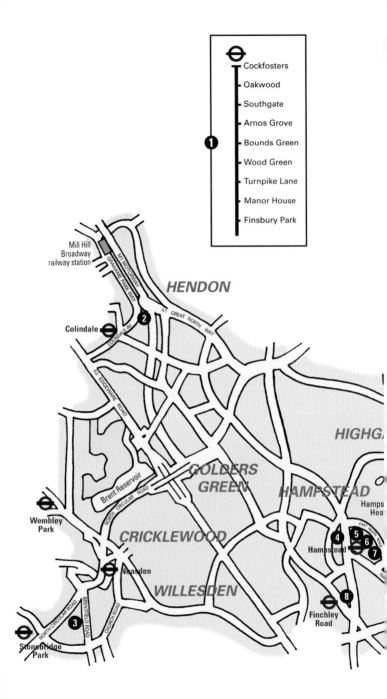

Cockfosters

Oakwood

Southgate

Arnos Grove

Bounds Green

Wood Green

Turnpike Lane

Manor House

Finsbury Park

Mill Hill
Broadway
railway station

Colindale

HENDON

M1 MOTORWAY

GRAHAME PARK WAY

A41 GREAT NORTH WAY

COLINDALE AV

A5 EDGWARE ROAD

HIGHGA

Wembley
Park

Brent Reservoir

NORTH CIRCULAR ROAD

GOLDERS
GREEN

HAMPSTEAD

Hamps
Hea

CRICKLEWOOD

Neasden

WILLESDEN

Hampstead

EAST HEATH ROAD

Stonebridge
Park

NORTH CIRCULAR ROAD

BRENTFIELD ROAD

CHURCH ROAD

Finchley
Road

CHAPTER 9

GREATER LONDON – NORTH

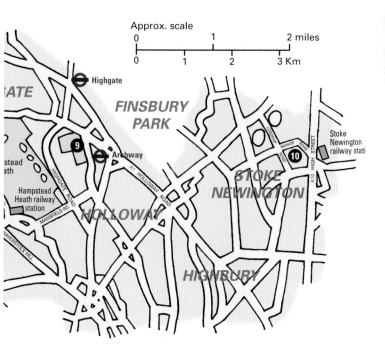

Address: On the Cockfosters extension of the Piccadilly Line, running from Manor House to Cockfosters.

Opening hours: Unrestricted access to station exteriors. The interiors can be seen when the tube is in operation, from around 5.30am to 1am.

Cost: Free to view from the outside, the usual tube fares to travel (see tfl.gov.uk/fares).

Transport: Piccadilly tube stations, as listed above.

Bounds Green

Cockfosters

Arnos Grove

Southgate

ART DECO TUBE STATIONS

London's tube system is more often associated with misery (overcrowding, delays, high prices and strikes) rather than anything associated with art or style. But step above ground, away from the crowds, heat and stress of tube travel, and some of the tube buildings are an architectural and aesthetic delight. This is notably the case with some of the work of Charles Holden (1875-1960), an English architect best known for designing London tube stations during the '20s and '30s. He designed around 50 in total, perhaps most famously the eight stations on the Cockfosters extension of the Piccadilly Line (dark blue on the map) on the route from Finsbury Park: Manor House, Turnpike Lane, Wood Green, Bounds Green, Arnos Grove, Southgate, Oakwood and Cockfosters.

The stations on the Cockfosters extension set new aesthetic standards, never before seen on London's Underground, and most are now Grade II listed. They're built in a range of modern, Art Deco styles, including boxes, circles, octagons, towers and other streamlined decorative touches.

Some of the eight are more striking than others. Cockfosters is more modestly designed than most, without the mass evident at Arnos Grove (built in a barrel-like style) and Oakwood (more conservatively rectangular in style), and lacking Southgate's sleek avant-garde elegance and style. Yet it still has appeal, a low rectangular structure, with squat square towers at each end.

Southgate is one of the best known of the many stations that Charles Holden designed, built in an Art Deco/Streamline Moderne style, a late Art Deco style that emerged in the '30s. A circular, drum-like ticket hall rises from the low structure, topped by a flat concrete roof. Its excellent state of preservation and original features – notably the escalators – make it a popular location for filming period dramas.

If you only see a couple of the eight stations, we recommend you choose Arnos Grove and Southgate (which, conveniently, are next to one another on the Piccadilly Line). They're attractive during the day, but even better at night and almost crying out to be photographed, when floodlighting beautifully displays and highlights their Art Deco features and shapes.

Address: Grahame Park Way, NW9 5LL (020-8205 2266, rafmuseum.org. uk/london).

Opening hours: Most exhibits are open daily, Nov-Feb, 10am to 4pm, Mar-Oct, 10am to 5pm, including most bank holidays.

Cost: Free, except for the 4D Theatre £5 (£16 for families of up to four people). Car park £5 (up to 7 hrs).

Transport: Colindale tube or Mill Hill Broadway rail.

RAF MUSEUM LONDON

Somewhat hidden away in an unfashionable north London suburb, on the site of Hendon's London Aerodrome (even though it's in Colindale not Hendon!), this free museum is one of the world's best flight exhibits. It's Britain's only national museum devoted wholly to aviation (split between this site and one at Cosford in the Midlands – hence the inclusion of 'London' in its name), housing over 100 aircraft from around the world, from early designs to modern jets and military aircraft.

The museum (opened in 1972) is housed in five huge buildings: the Grahame-White Factory & Watch Office; Milestones of Flight; Bomber Hall; Battle of Britain Hall; and Historic Hangers, plus the smaller Aeronautics Interactive Centre. It covers aviation history from early balloon flights to the latest jet fighters. Highlights include an early airship gondola, a Blériot from 1909, de Havilland Gypsy Moth, Sopwith Camel, Hawker Hurricane, Supermarine Spitfire, Messerschmitt 109, Harrier GR3, and the most up to date aircraft, the Eurofighter Typhoon.

An upper floor allows visitors to overlook the hangars in all their glory, while platforms allow you to get close to the aircraft. There are a number of interactive activities, including 4D cinema, an air traffic control simulator and 'Our Finest Hour', which uses film, audio and special lighting to recreate the atmosphere of the Battle of Britain. The Aeronauts Interactive Centre has over 40 'hands on' experiments, which help visitors learn how an aircraft flies. As well as these free interactive features, the new 4D cinema allows you to experience the feeling of flight.

The museum has a huge collection (around 250,000) of photographs, mostly black and white, while the library has tens of thousands of printed works from the 18th century to the present time. Original documents from the museum's archive and library collections can be consulted in the reading room and information is also provided by post, email and telephone. A film and sound collection boasts some 7m feet of film, dating from the pioneering days of flight (the earliest reel is from 1910) to the present day. For details of the photographic collection, library, and the film and sound collection, see the website. The museum also contains an art gallery, shop, café, licensed restaurant and picnic area.

Visitors should note that the museum is vast and it's difficult to take in everything in one visit. With this in mind, the website has a useful facility that helps you plan your visit and make the best use of your time, whether on a short or extended visit.

Address: BAPS Shri Swaminarayan Mandir, 105-119 Brentfield Rd, NW10 8LD (020-8965 2651, londonmandir.baps.org).

Opening hours: Daily, 9am to 6pm. Free guided tours (groups can book via the website). Restaurant: Mon-Fri, 10am to 8pm, Sat 10am to 10pm, Sun 10am to 9pm. Booking advisable. An exhibition 'Understanding Hinduism' and video explains how the temple was built and its significance, as well as telling the history of Hinduism.

Cost: Free. Exhibition £2 adults, £1.50 seniors and children.

Transport: Neasden, Stonebridge Pk or Wembley Pk tube.

NEASDEN TEMPLE

Included by *Readers Digest* in its list of 'the Seventy Wonders of the Modern World', this is one of London's unsung treasures, partly due to its location in an unglamorous part of northwest London. But its striking size, intricate design and warm, smiling worshippers make it well worth the trip (it attracts over 500,000 visitors a year).

It's full name is BAPS Shri Swaminarayan Mandir, London (popularly knows as the Neasden Temple), a place of worship or prayer for Hindus following a tradition dating back many millennia. The murtis and rituals of arti and worship in the mandir form the very core in elevating the soul to the pinnacle of God-realisation. Swaminarayan mandirs worldwide fulfil the lofty concept of the Hindu tradition of mandirs.

The website states that it's 'Europe's first traditional Hindu temple' and it's also said to be the largest of its kind outside India, 70ft high, covering 1.5 acres and topped by several pinnacles and five domes. The assembly hall can accommodate 5,000 people.

It was built according to the principles of ancient Indian Shilpashastras using traditional methods and materials. Its construction took just two years and included some 3,000 tons of the finest Bulgarian limestone and 2,000 tons of Italian Carrara marble, which was hand-carved in India into 26,300 pieces by 1,526 craftsmen and shipped to Britain for assembly. The website describes the temple as 'a masterpiece of Indian stonework and craftsmanship, replete with its towering white pinnacles, smooth domes and intricate marble pillars, all based on ancient Vedic principles of art and architecture'.

As it's a religious building, there are guidelines for visitors that should be observed, including no shorts or skirts above the knee; shoes must be removed before entering (so wear your best socks!); no photography inside the temple; mobile phones must be switched off and silence maintained; and those aged under 17 must be accompanied by an adult. A full list of guidelines is provided on the website.

As well as the monumental exterior, you can wander through the incredibly decorative, carving-encrusted interior, and there's a souvenir shop and one of London's best Indian vegetarian restaurants (Shayona). Perhaps the most striking impression you'll be left with is the warm welcome provided by the friendly, tranquil worshippers at this intriguing temple.

AT A GLANCE

Address: Hampstead Grove, NW3 6SP (020-7435 3471, nationaltrust.org.uk/fenton-house).

Opening hours: Mar-Oct: Wed-Sun, 11am to 4pm (check website for exact dates) plus selected days in Nov-Dec. Closed Jan-Feb.

Cost: £10 adults, £5 child, £25 family (2 adults). National Trust members free.

Transport: Hampstead tube.

FENTON HOUSE

Affluent, leafy Hampstead is full of sizeable, attractive properties and this is one of the earliest, largest and most architecturally important – a charming 17th-century merchant's house. It was built around 1686 and has been virtually unaltered over 300 years of continuous occupation. The large garden is also remarkably unchanged. *Country Life* magazine described it as 'London's most enchanting country house' and it's now owned by the National Trust. The Fentons, who bought the house in 1793, gave it the name and made some Regency alterations that give the house its current appearance.

The house is in a classic, almost idealised, Queen Anne style, of a type that has been copied by generations of dolls' house makers ever since. It stands back from the street, which gives it an air of tranquillity, and is built from elegant, deep brown brickwork, with red-rubbed brick for the dressings and an absence of carved stone. There are Doric pilasters around the door and a boldly carved wooden cornice under the eaves. The ground plan of the house is a perfect square cut into quarters by a cross. Two arms contain the staircases, the other two the hall and landings.

Fenton House is home to a collection of early keyboard instruments assembled by the many-named Major George Henry Benton Fletcher (1866-1944). He had a varied career as a soldier, social worker and archaeologist (who dug with the famous Flinders Petrie), and was also a perhaps unlikely instrument collector. One of them is sometimes played for visitors during opening hours.

The house also boasts collections of paintings (notably some fine portraits – artists represented in the collection include Jan Bruegel, Albrecht Durer, John Russell, Francis Sartorius and G. F. Watts), porcelain (there are world-class collections of English, European and Oriental porcelain), 17th-century needlework pictures and Georgian furniture (of the decorative and delicate sort).

The garden is laid out on the side of a hill and divided into upper and lower levels. It's an almost rural haven in a heavily populated part of London, noted for its sunken walled section, with a glasshouse, vegetable beds, culinary herb border and flower beds. There's also a 300-year-old orchard of agreeably gnarled apples trees, producing over 30 different varieties.

BURGH HOUSE & HAMPSTEAD MUSEUM

Leafy, upmarket Hampstead in north London is one of the capital's most desirable residential areas, much favoured by wealthy media executives and successful actors, writers, rock stars and other creative types. It's one of those districts that merits simply wandering around, soaking up the atmosphere, admiring the architecture and realising that you couldn't afford to rent a garage here, let alone buy a house.

It's eminently civilised, as is Burgh House, nestled in the heart of old Hampstead and home to the area's local museum. It wouldn't claim to be one of the capital's great collections, but it's varied and interesting, and, like so many of London's local displays, often passes under the radar – of local residents as well as visitors.

Burgh House is Grade I listed and was built in 1704 in the time of Queen Anne. It's a handsome building and one of the oldest houses in Hampstead, with original panelled rooms and staircase. It's named after a certain Reverend Allatson Burgh, a notably unpopular cleric, who bought it in 1822. Among its many tenants over the years was Rudyard Kipling's daughter, Elsie Bambridge, in the '30s.

The property is now used for a variety of purposes: as a local history museum, art gallery, classical music venue, shop and café. The museum's permanent display comprises over 3,000 objects, many relating to social history, fine art and notable Hampstead residents (and the area has played host to many). There's a display dedicated to the painter John Constable, who spent time in Hampstead (and is buried in St John-at-Hampstead graveyard), and to the poet John Keats, who lived in the area for a short time (see **Keats House** on page 279).

The museum traces Hampstead's long history, from prehistoric times to the present day. Hampstead Heath (around 800 acres of heathland, meadows and woodland, and one of the highest points in London) contains traces of Hampstead's earliest known inhabitants, Mesolithic hunters from around 7,000 BC, plus evidence of Bronze Age settlement.

Burgh House's Buttery Café attracts many locals who've probably never thought of visiting the museum. As well as a cosy indoor space, there are tables in the pretty garden which is full of nooks and crannies; a lovely place to sit with a coffee or a glass of wine in this most civilised part of London.

Address: 2 Willow Rd, NW3 1TH (020-7435 6166, nationaltrust.org.uk/2-willow-road).

Opening hours: Mar to early Nov, Wed-Sun, 11am to 3pm (see website for exact dates) and on some Mondays. Closed Jan-Feb and Nov-Dec. Entry by guided tour (40 mins) at 11am, noon, 1pm and 2pm. Bookings must be made via the website.

Cost: £9 adult, £4.50 child, £22.50 family (2 adults).

Transport: Hampstead tube.

GOLDFINGER'S HOUSE

A groundbreaking modernist home, designed in 1939 by the splendidly-named, Budapest-born architect Erno Goldfinger (1902-1987). It was home for him and his family (he married Ursula Blackwell, of the Crosse and Blackwell family, which some have suggested solved his financial problems) until his death in 1987. It's part of a terrace of three houses, 1-3 Willow Road, and is the largest of the three, managed by the National Trust (numbers 1 and 3 remain private homes).

A number of cottages were demolished to make way for the building of the three houses, which was strongly opposed by some local residents, including James Bond author Ian Fleming. It's said he developed a strong dislike of Goldfinger as a result, which led to him using the name Auric Goldfinger for one of his most famous villains. Certain people cite Fleming's supposed anti-Semitism as another, stronger reason. But things could have been even worse, as Goldfinger originally intended to build a block of flats with studios on the site (with one for his own family), but his plans were rejected by the London County Council.

The building is made from concrete faced with red brick, the external concrete frame allowing for a spacious interior uncluttered by supporting structures. It has an elegant, space-saving spiral staircase at its heart, designed by the Danish engineer Ove Arup. Large windows give a sense of light and space (crucial to Goldfinger's philosophy of how buildings should be), allowing panoramic views over Hampstead Heath. Carefully designed colour schemes impart different moods to various areas of the house, while ledges and recesses house works of art and interesting 'found' objects. Built-in cupboards preserve the purity of line in the house.

Goldfinger designed much of the house's furniture, which still has a contemporary air, and the property also houses his fine collection of modern art and personal possessions. The art collection is significant, including works by Marcel Duchamp, Max Ernst, Henry Moore and Bridget Riley.

Address: 10 Keats Grove, NW3 2RR (020-7332 3868, cityoflondon. gov.uk/things-to-do/attractions-museums-entertainment/keats-house, keatsfoundation.com/keats-house-hampstead).

Opening hours: Thu-Fri and Sun, 11am-1pm and 2-4pm. Check the opening hours before visiting and pre-book to guarantee entry.

Cost: £7.50 adult, £4.50 concession, 18 and under free. The garden can be visited free of charge and is a popular spot for summer picnics.

Transport: Hampstead Heath rail or Hampstead tube.

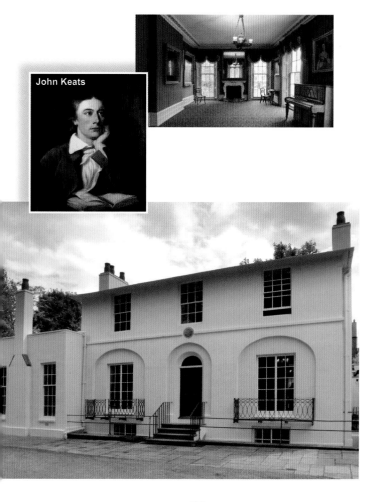

John Keats

KEATS HOUSE

This Grade I listed building is a shrine to one of the leading poets of the English Romantic movement (along with Lord Byron and Percy Bysshe Shelley), in a part of London long favoured by literary and creative types. John Keats (1795-1821) lived here for a mere 17 months from 1818, before travelling to Italy where he died of tuberculosis, aged just 25.

The house was built between 1814 and 1816, and was originally two separate properties, a pair of semi-detached houses with a shared garden called Wentworth Place. In 1838, the actress and one-time favourite of King George IV, Eliza Jane Chester, bought the property and knocked through to create one house.

John Keats lodged in one of the two properties with his friend Charles Brown, from December 1818 to September 1820, which although only a short period was perhaps his most productive. *Ode to a Nightingale* was allegedly written under a plum tree in the garden. He also found love here (appropriate for a member of the Romantic movement), in the form of Fanny Brawne, who lived with her family in the adjacent house.

Keats House has a large variety of Keats-related material, including books, paintings and household items. There are letters by Keats, books in which he wrote some of his poetry, the engagement ring that he gave to Fanny Brawne (he died before they could be married), busts and portraits of Keats, and three locks of his brown hair.

Various rooms in the house have been faithfully recreated as they would have been when lived in by Keats, Brown, the Brawnes and Eliza Chester. The attention to detail is impressive; for example, paint analysis has been used to determine the exact colours originally used on the walls.

The museum holds regular literary and poetry events (related not just to Keats's work, but to poetry in general), as well as regular talks and exhibitions about various aspects of life in Regency London, e.g. architecture, fashion and garden design. See website for details.

Address: 20 Maresfield Gardens, NW3 5SX (020-7435 2002, freud.org. uk).

Opening hours: Wed-Sun, 10.30am to 5pm. See website for holiday opening times.

Cost: £14 adults, £12 concessions, £9 young persons (students, children 12-16.), under-12s free.

Transport: Finchley Rd tube.

Sigmund Freud

FREUD MUSEUM

The address says Hampstead, but this is the western reaches of that leafy district, hence the nearest tube. As a result, it's slightly 'off the map' and sometimes ignored. But it's an interesting, atmospheric museum, housed in what was the home of Sigmund Freud and his family when they fled the Nazi annexation of Austria in 1938. Built in 1920 in Queen Anne style, it's a large, red-brick house, striking and handsome as befits this upmarket part of London.

The house remained the Freud family home until 1982, when Anna Freud, Sigmund's youngest daughter (he had six children), died. Sigmund Freud himself didn't have the chance to live in the house for very long, dying a few weeks after the Second World War broke out in September 1939.

In view of the chaos of the late '30s, the Freuds were lucky to be able to bring their furniture and household effects to London, including lovely Biedermeier chests, tables and cupboards, and a collection of 18th- and 19th-century Austrian painted country furniture. Their possessions include a drawing of Freud by Salvador Dali (the Surrealists were strongly influenced by his writings).

The museum's centrepiece is Freud's study, preserved as it was during his lifetime, and exactly as it had been in Vienna: Freud wrote down the position of everything so that it could be faithfully recreated. The most famous exhibit is his psychoanalytic couch, on which all his patients reclined. It's covered with a richly coloured Iranian rug with chenille cushions piled on top.

The study also displays his impressive collection of antiquities (Egyptian, Greek, Roman and Oriental), totalling almost 2,000 items. Freud stated that his passion for collecting was second only to his addiction to cigars, and he sometimes used archaeology as a metaphor for psychoanalysis. The walls of the study are lined with shelves containing his large library of books.

The house also contains much from the life and works of Anna Freud, who lived here for 44 years and continued her father's psychoanalytic work, notably with children. Both she and Sigmund loved the garden (he was particularly fond of flowers), which is beautifully maintained, much as Freud would have known it. There's also a shop, selling many things Freud-related, and the museum hosts a series of courses, films and lectures about subjects relevant to Freud and to psychoanalysis in general.

AT A GLANCE

Address: Swains Lane, Highgate, N6 6QJ.

Opening hours: Unrestricted access to property exteriors, but they're privately owned homes and therefore entry to the interiors isn't possible.

Cost: Free.

Transport: Archway or Highgate tube.

HOLLY VILLAGE

Sitting in the elegant north London enclave of Highgate – beloved of pop stars and media types – Holly Village is of architectural and historical significance, being the first example of a gated housing development and built in an elaborate Gothic style. It's Grade II listed and close to Parliament Hill and attractive Highgate Village.

Holly Village is a group of eight buildings built around a spacious, tree-dotted green, comprising four detached houses and four pairs of adjoining cottages, i.e. 12 dwellings. They were built in 1865, designed by the architect Henry Astley Darbishire (who designed some of the first flats built by the great Victorian philanthropist George Peabody) for Baroness Angela Burdett-Coutts, one of Victorian England's wealthiest women. She was the granddaughter of Thomas Coutts, founder of the exclusive bank (to the Queen, among others), and helped to manage the bank as well as being involved in philanthropic work. The Baroness was also well connected, a friend of Dickens (who was involved in planning Holly Village and called her 'my dearest friend'), Disraeli and Gladstone.

Holly Village would have been visible from Holly Lodge, the Burdett-Coutts' magnificent country villa on Highgate's West Hill (now demolished). It was, however, apparently not a work of philanthropy designed to house the poor and the needy, but was a commercial venture with high rents, although there's some disagreement over this.

Certainly, no expense was spared in its construction. Top quality teak wood and Portland stone were used, and Italian craftsmen were employed for the exterior wood carving. The building façades are ornate, picturesque and imaginative, with contrast patterns in the walls, crenellations, pinnacles, dormers, and small heads and animals (Burdett-Coutts was an animal lover, involved in the founding of the RSPCA). There are sculptures by Burdett-Coutts herself on either side of the elaborate entrance archway gate, being idealised, classically-robed representations of Burdett-Coutts and her long-time friend Hannah Brown. Burdett-Coutts holds a dog, Brown a dove. The diamond-shaped Coutts coat-of-arms appears prominently in Portland stone on each building.

Holly Village is a fine, unique example of Victorian Gothic in a residential complex, although it's too detailed and overdone for some modern tastes. And it probably has a touch of *Stepford Wives* about it; very suburban perfect, perhaps with vaguely creepy undertones, accentuated by its atmospheric location close to Highgate cemetery.

AT A GLANCE

Address: 215 Stoke Newington High St, N16 0LH (020-7275 7557,
abney-park.org.uk, abneypark.org).

Opening hours: Daily, 8am to dusk.

Cost: Free.

Transport: Stoke Newington rail.

ABNEY PARK CEMETERY

Now a memorial park and woodland nature reserve run by Abney Park Trust, Abney Park Cemetery was one of London's 'Magnificent Seven' garden cemeteries, built between 1832 and 1841 by the Victorians to cope with London's rapid population increase. The other six were Brompton, Highgate, Kensal Green (see page 47), Nunhead (see page 297), Tower Hamlets and West Norwood.

Abney Park was originally laid out in the early 18th century on the instructions of Lady Mary Abney and others. In 1840 it became a non-denominational garden cemetery, but also a semi-public arboretum and educational institute. It was set out in an entirely different way from the other Magnificent Seven and had a wider purpose that was rather ahead of its time. It was the first wholly non-denominational garden cemetery in Europe, and was specifically designed using motifs not associated with contemporary religion. For example, it has an impressive entrance in the then-popular Egyptian revival style, designed by William Hosking, the first professor of architecture at Kings College, London, who also designed the Grade II listed Abney Park Chapel.

The park's arboretum was originally designed as a labelled tree collection for educational walks, and much enhanced the wooded character of the park, which already had several exotic trees from various far flung places, some planted in the 1690s. The planting of the original 2,500 arboretum trees and shrubs was designed to be botanical and naturalistic, rather than purely aesthetic, which led Abney Park to become regarded as the most impressively landscaped garden cemetery of its time.

Burial rights in the park ceased in 1978, and it's now dedicated to a wide range of projects in the fields of arts, education, nature conservation and recreation. However, ashes can be scattered at certain locations and there's still the occasional discretionary or courtesy burial.

Today, the park is a romantic wilderness and bolthole in a grittily urban part of London, every bit as atmospheric and interesting as the much better-known Highgate Cemetery (another of the Magnificent Seven). It's wild and crumbling state adds to its charm and interest, with some magnificent urns, inscriptions, plinths, ivy-clad statues and sculptures – many in a terrible state – leaning, tumbling and falling over, and merging with the planting. The most famous 'resident' is William Booth, founder of the Salvation Army, who lies beneath a huge, striking headstone. The park is full of atmospheric walks and picnic spots, and rich in wildlife.

CHAPTER 10

GREATER LONDON – SOUTH

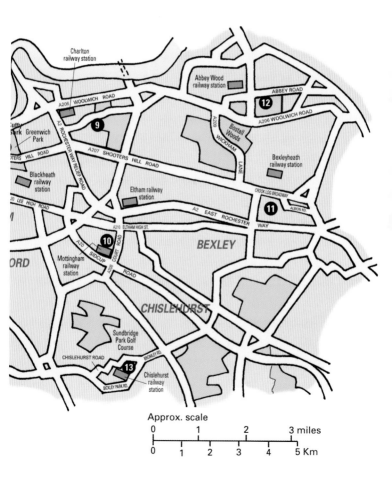

Charlton railway station

Abbey Wood railway station

ABBEY ROAD

A206 WOOLWICH ROAD

12

A206 WOOLWICH ROAD

A209

Bostall Woods

WICKHAM LANE

9

A2 ROCHESTER WAY RELIEF ROAD

A207 SHOOTERS HILL ROAD

Cutty Park

Greenwich Park

SHOOTERS HILL ROAD

Bexleyheath railway station

Blackheath railway station

A20 LEE HIGH ROAD

Eltham railway station

CROOK LOG BROADWAY

A2 EAST ROCHESTER WAY

ALBION RD.

11

A210 ELTHAM HIGH ST.

BEXLEY

A20

10

SIDCUP

COURT ROAD

Mottingham railway station

A20

ROAD

FORD

CHISLEHURST

Sundbridge Park Golf Course

CHISLEHURST ROAD

BROMLEY RD.

13

Chislehurst railway station

BICKLEY PARK RD.

Approx. scale

| 0 | | 1 | | 2 | | 3 miles |

| 0 | 1 | 2 | 3 | 4 | 5 Km |

Address: 50-60 Mitcham Rd, SW17 9NA (020-8672 5717, buzzbingo. com/club/tooting.html).

Opening hours: Daily 10am to 4am.

Cost: Admission is to members only (free to over-18s). See website or telephone for details of how to join. Various fees for bingo games.

Transport: Tooting Broadway tube or Tooting and Earlsfield rail.

BUZZ BINGO CLUB

The south London district of Tooting is probably best known by Britons of a certain age as the setting for the '70s situation comedy Citizen Smith, whose hero, a beret-wearing, wannabe-Communist called Wolfie Smith, founded a fictional revolutionary organisation, the Tooting Popular Front, and popularised the cry 'Freedom for Tooting'.

But it's also home to an exotic treasure of 20th-century architecture – formerly the Granada Tooting cinema – which is the ultimate British example of the 'super cinema style' of the '30s. It has been called a world class cinema and undoubtedly has the most lavishly-decorated interior of any British cinema (and one of the most exotic in the world). What is today the Buzz Bingo Club was commissioned by Sidney Bernstein, who later founded Granada Television, and opened in 1931 as a cinema called the Granada Theatre, also acting as a concert venue. It became a bingo hall in the '70s.

It was built in a Moderne Italianate style (an Art Deco style) by the English theatre and cinema architect Cecil Masey, with a towering entrance and four tall pillars topped by Corinthian capitals. But it's the interior that's the notable part and the reason that it's regarded as Britain's most spectacular cinema.

The interior was designed by the noted Russian state set designer (and prince) Theodore Komisarjevsky in a style (or styles) that's intriguingly difficult to pin down. It's both Gothically medieval – sometimes known as 'Shakespearean Gothic' – and was also influenced by the Moorish designs of the Alhambra Palace in Granada, Spain.

The interior includes a foyer with columns, a grand staircase, a hall of mirrors and Gothic arcading. Grecian windows cast strobes of coloured light on the polished floors and there are cathedral porches, heraldic symbols, glass chandeliers and murals of medieval-like musicians and damsels. It's a visual treat, which is somewhat at odds with the fact that the majority of its current users ignore the dizzying sights around them, preferring to bend their heads in concentration over their bingo cards.

However, this glorious building's past usage was rather more glamorous than bingo. As well as being a cinema, complete with a Wurlitzer organ, the old Granada Tooting played host to a range of stars from various eras, including Frank Sinatra, Lena Horne, Johnny Ray, Frankie Laine, Danny Kaye, Little Richard, The Beatles, The Rolling Stones and Jimi Hendrix. It used to be Grade II listed, but was upgraded in 2000 to Grade I, the first '30s cinema building to receive such an honour.

AT A GLANCE

Address: **Bellenden Rd, Peckham, SE15 4QY.**
Opening hours: **Unrestricted access.**
Cost: **Free.**
Transport: **Peckham Rye rail.**

BELLENDEN RENEWAL AREA

The Bellenden Renewal Area is part of a wider Peckham Renewal Project. It was instigated in 2003-2004 to help improve and renovate Peckham, a rundown part of south London made famous (or infamous) in Britain as the setting of a long-running situation comedy, *Only Fools and Horses*. Its central character, Del Boy, was a borderline-criminal, small-time market trader living in a tower block on a rough estate, and this has coloured many people's perceptions of Peckham (which partly explains the need for an image makeover).

The focus of this has been Bellenden Road, which has been gentrified and transformed from an undesirable inner city area to an attractive urban village, with bistros, bookshops, boutiques and cafés, creating a bohemian café culture vibe. But the most obvious improvement to Bellenden Road has been the addition of various kinds of street furniture, designed by a variety of famous artists and designers, with funding provided jointly by Southwark Council and a private body. The area hasn't (yet) been transformed into a middle class haven like Hampstead or Dulwich, but it's much improved, while still retaining a certain edge (rather than its previous air of deprivation and simmering violence).

The street art is highly appropriate, as the area has long attracted artists, with Camberwell and Goldsmiths art colleges nearby. And two of the designers of the Bellenden street furniture, Anthony Gormley and Tom Phillips, have studios in Peckham, while another, Zandra Rhodes, has one in nearby Bermondsey. Anthony Gormley is a sculptor, best known for his monumental *Angel of the North* (see also **Thameside Sculptures** on page 253). Zandra Rhodes is a veteran fashion designer, probably known as much for her bright clothes and coiffure as for her designs, while artist Tom Phillips falls into the category of 'sometime Royal Academy *enfant terrible*'.

The street furniture consists of bollards in black, bronze, pink and rust, designed by Anthony Gormley and Zandra Rhodes. Street lights with Charles Rennie Mackintosh-like designs are by Tom Phillips, who also designed arches, gates, pavements and wall mosaics, while there's an 'exploding shop window book' by John Latham. Local artist Helen Harrison designed exotic play areas and park sculptures, while Zandra Rhodes has given the area lively pink bus shelters (pink is one of her signature colours). Modernist ironwork gates (on churches, houses and schools) are by local artist Heather Burrell

Address: Gallery Rd, SE21 7AD (020-8693 5254, dulwichpicturegallery.org.uk).

Opening hours: Wed-Sun, 10am to 5pm. Closed Mon-Tue except bank holidays. Gardens: Tue-Sat, 8am to 6pm, Sun 9am to 6pm. Café: Tue-Sat, 8am-5pm, Sun 9am to 5pm.

Cost: £15 adults, £8 concessions (disabled, unemployed, students), £5 under 30s, free under 18s. Tickets must be booked online.

Transport: W Dulwich or N Dulwich rail.

Rembrant self-portrait

DULWICH PICTURE GALLERY

The tranquil south London suburb of Dulwich is home to a quietly revolutionary art gallery. Built by Sir John Soane (a noted architect, most famous for designing the Bank of England and for his museum – see page 111) and opened in 1817, the Dulwich Picture Gallery was England's first purpose-built, public art gallery, and has proved highly influential on the way we view art.

The collection itself was mainly bequeathed by successful art dealers Francis Bourgeois and Noel Deschamps. They originally assembled it between 1790 and 1795 for the King of Poland, who planned to establish a national gallery in Warsaw. But when Poland was partitioned the plans were shelved and Bourgeois and Deschamps eventually left the collection to the British public, to be housed in a specially-built gallery. It's thought that Sir John Soane was chosen to design it as he was a friend of Bourgeois.

Soane's design, a series of simple interlinked rooms lit by natural light via overhead skylights, has been a major influence on the design of art galleries ever since. He cleverly designed the skylights to illuminate the paintings indirectly, to avoid damaging them with direct light. As the noted 20th-century architect Philip Johnson said, 'Soane has taught us how to display paintings'.

The building itself is beautiful – the world's most beautiful art gallery, according to some – an elegant study of abstract classicism, made from brick with Portland stone detailing. A modern extension, designed by Rick Mather, was built in 1999. The gallery is surrounded by tranquil gardens, mainly lawns, with a number of unusual trees, some over 200 years old. The gallery has a shop and café, and runs an extensive series of lectures and other educational events.

As for the collection itself, the gallery houses one of the world's most important collections of European old master paintings from the 17th and 18th centuries, including many of the highest quality. It's especially rich in French, Italian and Spanish Baroque paintings, and in British portraits from Tudor times to the 19th century. It includes works by Canaletto, Constable, Gainsborough, Hogarth, Landseer, Murillo, Poussin, Raphael, Rembrandt, Reynolds, Rubens and Van Dyck. You can search and display the works via the website.

The gallery regularly stages temporary exhibitions, which are often significant; these have included Canaletto in England, Paul Nash: The Elements, Norman Rockwell's America, and Twombly and Poussin – Arcadian Painters.

HORNIMAN MUSEUM

I t's well worth journeying out to the southern suburbs to see this interesting and varied collection. It opened in 1901 in a lovely Arts and Crafts and Art Nouveau-style building designed by Charles Harrison Townsend, who was also responsible for the striking Whitechapel Art Gallery (see page 231). The museum was founded by the Victorian tea trader Frederick John Horniman (1835-1906) to house his superb collection of cultural artefacts, ethnography, natural history and musical instruments, some collected personally on his travels (although he didn't leave Britain until he was 60), but most accumulated by his tea merchants.

The collection runs to 350,000 objects in total (over the past century, the museum has added significantly to the original bequest). The Horniman's exhibits aren't dusty or static and the collection is constantly being extended, researched and brought into public view. The ethnography and music collections have designated status; i.e. are considered of great importance. The ethnography collection is the third most significant in the UK after the British Museum and the Pitt-Rivers Museum (Oxford). The earliest musical instrument dates from 1500BC (a pair of bone clappers in the form of human hands, made in Egypt).

The museum is noted for its large collection of stuffed animals and has one of London's oldest aquariums, noted for its unique design (there's a new, modern aquarium in the basement). There are also some interesting archaeological exhibits, from Africa, America, Asia, Europe and the Pacific, including much British prehistoric material, some of it from significant sites, e.g. Grimes Graves and Swanscombe. The detailed website contains comprehensive information about the various collections.

The Horniman is set in 16 acres of award-winning, beautifully maintained gardens, which include a Grade II listed conservatory, bandstand, animal enclosure, nature trail and an ornamental garden. A 20ft (6.1m) totem pole (dating from 1985) sits outside the museum's main entrance, and is one of the UK's few totem poles. There's also a grass-roofed 'Centre for Understanding the Environment' building, constructed from sustainable materials.

After visiting the museum, it's worth taking a stroll to Ringmore Rise (a road) behind the museum, from where you can enjoy wonderful panoramic views of central London.

Address: Linden Grove, SE15 3LP (020-7525 2000, southwark.gov.uk/parks-and-open-spaces/parks/nunhead-cemetery).

Opening hours: Apr-Sep, daily 8.30am to 7pm; Oct, daily 8.30am to 5pm; Nov-Feb, daily 8.30am to 4pm; Mar, daily 8.30am to 5pm (see website for exact dates). The Friends of Nunhead Cemetery (see fonc.org.uk) organise tours (1½ to 2 hrs) on the last Sun of the month (2pm from Linden Grove entrance).

Cost: Free.

Transport: Nunhead rail.

NUNHEAD CEMETERY

Consecrated in 1840, Nunhead Cemetery is one of the 'magnificent seven' Victorian cemeteries built in a ring around London's outskirts. According to the Friends of Nunhead Cemetery it's 'perhaps the least known but most attractive of the great Victorian cemeteries of London'. Southwark Council regards it as 'one of Southwark's hidden treasures'.

The cemeteries were built in response to a massive surge in London's population in the first half of the 19th century, when it more than doubled, from 1m to 2.3m. The city's small parish churchyards quickly became dangerously overcrowded, with grim consequences: decaying corpses got into the water supply, causing a number of epidemics. As a result, seven large cemeteries were built between 1832 and 1841, the other six being Abney Park (see page 285), Brompton, Highgate, Kensal Green (see page 47), Tower Hamlets and West Norwood.

The new cemeteries appealed to the growing middle class, which was eager to distance itself from the working class and to demonstrate its status. Graves were regarded as a visible part of a family's property. Nunhead is the second-largest of the seven, covering 52 acres, with monumental entrance and lodges designed by James Bunstone Bunning.

Much of it is crumbling and wild – locals call it a nature reserve or wilderness – and it's certainly a tranquil place for a walk. Funding from the Heritage Lottery Fund and Southwark Council has helped with its restoration, along with the efforts of the Friends of Nunhead Cemetery, but many people see Nunhead's wilderness element as fundamental to its appeal. Weathered gravestones and tumbling statuary peer through extravagant under- and overgrowth and weed-choked paths, and the cemetery is full of interesting contrasts, e.g. between some magnificent monuments in memory of the era's most prominent citizens and the modest, small headstones erected for common people, and between the formal, elegant avenue of tall lime trees and the many smaller pathways, some of which resemble country lanes.

The cemetery has become an important haven for flora and fauna, and offers some great views over London. At its highest point it's around 200ft (60m) above sea level and commands vistas stretching from the towers of Canary Wharf westwards as far as the London Eye near the Houses of Parliament.

AT A GLANCE

Address: Ben Pimlott Building, Goldsmiths College, University of London, New Cross, SE14 6NW (virtualtours.gold.ac.uk/map/highlights/ben-pimlott-building-scribble).

Opening hours: Unrestricted access.

Cost: Free.

Transport: New Cross rail.

THE GOLDSMITHS SCRIBBLE

Even its most die-hard devotees wouldn't claim that New Cross is one of London's loveliest areas. It has its strengths, being vibrant, low-cost and close to the heart of London, but few people would disagree that it deserves and needs some brightening up, and this example of outdoor art makes a decent stab at it.

The Scribble sits atop the Ben Pimlott Building, a purpose-built (2005), seven-storey teaching space in the New Cross campus of the famous Goldsmiths College (part of the University of London), that specialises in teaching creative and cultural subjects, most famously art. It describes itself as 'the incubator of British art at a time when the UK leads contemporary art throughout the world'.

The most notable feature of the building is a huge, 30-foot high, 27-ton sculpture known as *The Scribble*, which sits on the fifth floor terrace. It was designed by the architect and artist Will Alsop (whose firm, Alsop and Partners – then Alsop Architects – also designed the building), who described it as 'a slightly irreverent take on the college's irrepressible creative urges'. Goldsmiths' alumni are a heady mix of British creative talent, including Anthony Gormley, Damien Hirst, Malcolm McLaren, Mary Quant and Bridget Riley, none of whom are to everyone's taste, but are certainly influential.

The Scribble is a metallic spaghetti structure, made from 229 pieces of steel, of which 131 were assembled on site. If stretched out, it would be 1,752ft (534m) long (over twice the height of the 800ft/244m Canary Wharf Tower), with 72 twists. It's not to everybody's liking, but what art is? Some critics think that it's trying too hard, in a 'look at us, we're creative' sort of way, and regard it as arty rather than artistic.

But it also has many supporters, as does the building, which has an industrial aesthetic to reflect the studio space within. Three sides of the building are clad in metal, the fourth is glazed, which floods it with natural light. The structure has three external elements: an external escape staircase, *The Scribble*, and artwork on the south, east and west façades. These serve to add visual interest and also to break up the scale of the metal elevations, and cast changing shadows across the façades. This makes the building visually attractive in different ways in different weather conditions, and it's also floodlit at night to interesting effect.

Address: Trinity Laban, 30 Creekside, Deptford, SE8 3DZ (020-8305 4444, trinitylaban.ac.uk, tours@trinitylaban.ac.uk).

Opening hours: Unrestricted access to the exterior (which is the main attraction). See the website for performances, events and guided tours.

Cost: Free to view the exterior and the interior's public areas. There's a fee for guided tours.

Transport: Deptford or Greenwich rail or Cutty Sark DLR.

TRINITY LABAN

To see one of London's most lauded and interesting modern buildings, head to Deptford (but rapidly becoming gentrified), a once down-at-heel area of riverside on the Thames's south bank. This luminous structure claims to be 'the largest purpose-built contemporary dance space in the world' and was named after Hungarian choreographer, dancer and teacher, Rudolf Laban.

It was designed by Swiss architects Herzog and Meuron (in collaboration with visual artist Michael Craig-Martin), best known for turning Bankside power station into the Tate Modern (which has become one of the world's most visited art galleries) and for designing the striking stadium for the 2008 Beijing Olympics. The Laban won the prestigious Stirling Prize for Architecture in 2003, awarded by the Royal Institute of British Architects (RIBA).

The curved building occupies a 2-acre site overlooking Deptford Creek and includes a 300-seat dance theatre, studios, rehearsal space, lecture rooms, a library and a café. It's noted for its semi-translucent, polycarbonate cladding (punctuated by large, clear windows), which allows the dance and movement inside to be seen from outside as moving shadows through the walls. The cladding cloaks the building in shades of lime, magenta and turquoise, and at night it becomes a sort of coloured beacon, with the light and movement illuminating the surrounding area and along Deptford Creek. (The Creekside area is also worth visiting, an interesting blend of houseboats, artists' studios, abandoned industrial sites and wildlife habitats – for more information, see creeksidecentre.org.uk.)

The building was designed ecologically; for example, nesting facilities for redstarts were built into the roof. It was also intended to be a catalyst to help rebrand and regenerate what has long been a neglected, run-down area. In 2005, Laban merged with the Trinity College of Music to become Trinity Laban, the UK's first Conservatoire of Music and Dance.

A number of the building's areas are accessible to the public (see above) and guided architectural tours are also available, which last around an hour. However, the exterior is the main attraction.

Address: **Chesterfield Walk, Blackheath, SE10 8QX (0370-333 1181, english-heritage.org.uk/visit/places/rangers-house-the-wernher-collection).**

Opening hours: **Apr-Sep (see website for exact dates), Wed-Sun, 11am to 4pm. Mon-Tue closed. Bookings can be made online but aren't mandatory. Closed Oct-Mar.**

Cost: **£10 adults, £9 concessions, £6 children (5-17), £26 family (2 adults and up to 3 children). English heritage members free.**

Transport: **Blackheath rail.**

THE RANGER'S HOUSE & WERNHER COLLECTION

The Ranger's House is an elegant, medium-sized, red brick Georgian villa built in the Palladian style, adjacent to Greenwich Park. The house dates from the early 1700s, a graceful building with panelled interiors, now managed by English Heritage. It was first used as the official residence of the Ranger of Greenwich Park in 1816, when it was called Chesterfield House.

The building alone is worth visiting, but all the more so because since 2002 it has housed the Wernher Collection of works of art (jewels, paintings, porcelain, silver and more), collected in the late 19th and early 20th centuries by German-born railway engineer's son Sir Julius Wernher (1850-1912). He made his fortune mining diamonds in South Africa – the company he formed was later amalgamated with De Beers, and he left over £11m when he died – and had a lifelong passion for collecting.

It's an unusual collection, of international importance, one of the best private collections of art assembled by one person, including some of Europe's most spectacular jewellery. This makes it all the more surprising that it has such a low profile; in fact, few people seem to have heard of it.

Nearly 700 works of art are on display, spread over 12 rooms, including early religious paintings, Dutch Old Masters, tiny carved Gothic ivories, fine renaissance bronzes and silver treasures. They demonstrate the many skills of medieval craftsmen and the quality of renaissance decorative arts. There are paintings by Francesco Francia, John Hoppner, Filippino Lippi, Hans Memling, Gabriel Metsu, George Romney, Sir Joshua Reynolds and others. The largest part of the collection is a varied mix of decorative art, including renaissance jewellery, medieval art, Byzantine and renaissance ivories, tapestries, furniture, Sevres porcelain, woodcarving and statues.

Wernher lived at Bath House in Piccadilly, London (and Luton Hoo in Bedfordshire), and some of the rooms at the Ranger's House have been decorated and arranged in such a way as to reflect how the collection would have originally been displayed when it was at Bath House. It's a notably varied collection (for which the word – now a cliché – 'eclectic' seems to have been invented), with something to interest and delight most visitors.

CHARLTON HOUSE

Charlton House is one of London's least-known architectural gems, a magnificent Jacobean mansion improbably situated in unfashionable Charlton. It commands an impressive site on a hill overlooking lawns and trees, at the heart of Charlton village, one of the few areas of southeast London to have kept its distinctive village features, including a parish church, part of the village green and the village main street.

Charlton House, the village's manor house, dominates the area, and if you stand outside it and gaze towards the village, you get a distinct flavour of an earlier age and a whiff of what life was like in one of London's old villages (reason enough to visit). All this is within sight of the iconic modern skyscrapers of Canary Wharf across the river.

It's one of several English houses called Charlton House, but is the most prominent and regarded as London's best-preserved Jacobean house and one of England's finest examples of Jacobean domestic architecture. The Jacobean phase of architecture (1603-1625) forms a link between the expansive Tudor style and the tidy, geometrical style associated with Inigo Jones.

Charlton House was built between 1607 and 1612 from red brick with stone dressing, with an 'E'-plan layout. It was built for Sir Adam Newton (who's buried across the road in St Luke's Church), Dean of Durham and tutor to Prince Henry, son of James I and elder brother of the future Charles I. Prince Henry died the year the house was completed.

The architect is unknown, but is thought to be John Thorpe. The orangery (later a public lavatory, but no longer used) is possibly the work of Inigo Jones. Charlton House was acquired by Greenwich Council in 1925 and later converted into a public library and community centre. The house, stables, orangery and park are intact except for the house's north wing, which was destroyed in the Second World War and later rebuilt.

An ancient mulberry tree in the garden was apparently planted at the suggestion of James I in 1608, making it probably the oldest in England. He was keen to develop a silk industry, but his plans turned into something of a joke: he planted a large mulberry garden on the land where Buckingham Palace was later built, but the delightfully unpredictable English climate killed it off (and, embarrassingly, they were in any case the wrong type of mulberry for breeding silkworms!).

AT A GLANCE

Address: Court Yd, Eltham, Greenwich, SE9 5QE (0370-333 1181, english-heritage.org.uk/visit/places/eltham-palace-and-gardens).

Opening hours: From Apr-Oct (see website for exact dates), daily, 10am to 5pm. See website for 'winter' opening times. Bookings can be made online but aren't mandatory.

Cost: £16 adults, £14.30 concessions, £9.60 children, £41.80 families (2 adults, 3 children).

Transport: Eltham or Mottingham rail.

ELTHAM PALACE

Eltham in suburban southeast London boasts a treat of a building that unexpectedly combines one of England's best Art Deco interiors with one of the few significant English medieval royal palaces with substantial remains – yet many people haven't even heard of Eltham Palace, let alone visited it. They might have seen it on screen, however, as it's a popular location with film and television directors.

Initially a moated manor house set in extensive parkland, the original palace was given to Edward II in 1305 and was a royal residence from the 14th to 16th centuries, including for Henry VIII in his younger days. It was eclipsed by the rebuilding of nearby Greenwich Palace – which was more easily accessible from the Thames – but hunting deer in its enclosed parks remained popular. These parks were almost stripped of trees and deer during the English Civil War (1642-1651), while the palace and its chapel were badly damaged.

The current building dates from the '30s, when Sir Stephen and Lady Courtauld were granted a lease. They restored the Great Hall, which boasts England's third-largest hammer-beam roof, gave it a minstrels' gallery, and incorporated it into a sumptuous home with a striking interior in a variety of Art Deco styles. Among many notable features are Lady Courtauld's gold-plated mosaic bathroom and the stunning circular entrance hall, the work of the Swedish designer Rolf Engströmer. The latter boasts an impressive glazed dome that floods it with light, highlighting elegant blackbean veneer and lush, figurative parquetry.

The red brick and Bath stone exterior is modelled on Wren's work at Hampton Court Palace, and parts of medieval buildings remain in and around the extensive gardens, as does a 15th-century bridge across the 14th-century moat (planted with lilies). The gardens are an added attraction – and ideal picnic spot – an important example of '30s garden design, and attractively dotted with medieval ruins and features.

The palace has a number of quirks, including three escape tunnels, which emerge in various parts of Eltham, under-floor heating, piped music and a centralised vacuum-cleaning system. As for the Courtaulds, they had a pet lemur (what else?), which apparently had free run of the house, as well as its own upstairs room, with a hatch leading downstairs. The Courtaulds departed in 1944 and the property passed to the Royal Army Educational Corps, who remained there until 1992. Eltham Palace was acquired by English Heritage in 1995, and major repairs and restoration of the interiors and gardens were completed four years later, along with the inevitable café and gift shop.

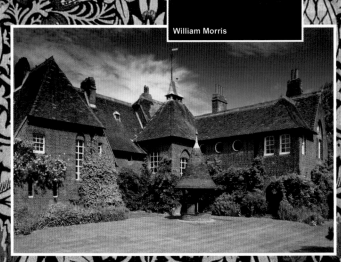

William Morris

THE RED HOUSE

You sometimes have to travel for your pleasures, and that's the case here. This important architectural gem and shrine for William Morris followers is situated in the borough of Bexley. It's bland commuterland, beyond the reach of London Underground (like much of southeast London), and is a 35-minute train ride from Charing Cross, plus a 15-minute stroll from Bexleyheath railway station. But the journey is surely worthwhile to see a building described by the Pre-Raphaelite painter Dante Gabriel Rossetti as 'more a poem than a house' and by the designer and artist Edward Burne-Jones as 'the beautifullest place on earth'.

It was designed by the architect Philip Webb and William Morris, founder of the Arts and Crafts movement, an international design movement instigated by Morris and inspired by the writings of the critic John Ruskin, which was influential in the late 19th and early 20th centuries. Morris and his family lived in the Red House for five years from 1860, only giving it up for financial reasons (he never returned).

The building is a significant landmark in English domestic architecture, and became a base for artists and craftsmen, being designed as both a home and an artists' workshop. It's regarded as an embodiment of the aesthetic principles that Morris upheld, and is a clever blend of the practical and the romantic, with Gothic and medieval influences.

The Red House is a large, elegant building, made of warm, red bricks and with substantial chimneys, a tall, steep tiled roof, diverse window styles and a beautiful stairway, making it striking both externally and internally. It retains plenty of Arts and Crafts features – original and restored – including furniture designed by William Morris and Philip Webb, and stained glass and paintings by Edward Burne-Jones (which might, perhaps, lead to accusations of bias regarding the earlier quotation).

The garden is also significant, intended to work in harmony with the building, or 'to clothe the house'. It was one of the first gardens to be designed as a series of rooms – extensions of the house – which were originally a herb garden, a vegetable garden, and two gardens of traditional British flowers and fruit trees.

The Red House is Grade I listed and was a private home until 2003, when it was acquired by the National Trust and subsequently opened to the public. Almost inevitably, it has a tea-room and gift shop.

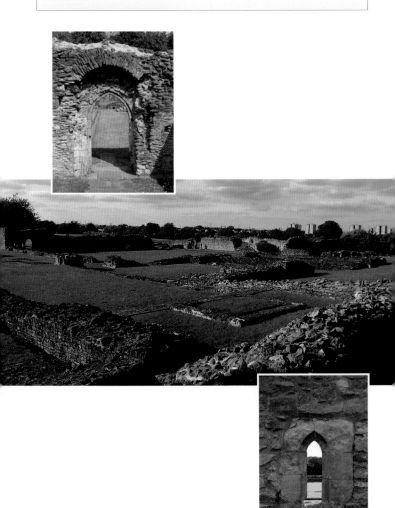

LESNES ABBEY

Another of southeast London's unexpectedly rich sites, Lesnes Abbey is a ruined Norman monastery in Abbey Wood, an area named after the 200 acres of woods adjacent to the abbey ruins. The abbey is a scheduled national monument (a nationally important archaeological or historic site), while the surrounding ancient woodland, park and heathland (one of Greater London's few remaining heaths) is a Site of Special Scientific Interest.

The abbey surrounds have several attractions, including Bronze Age burial mounds, a 55m-year-old fossil bank (noted for sharks' teeth and sea shells) and glorious spring displays of bluebells and daffodils. An old mulberry tree on the site is reputed to be one of those commissioned by King James I, who wanted to establish a silk industry. (However, silk moth caterpillars feed on the white mulberry, and the trees that the king was sold were black mulberries!)

The abbey was founded in 1178 as the Abbey of St Mary and St Thomas the Martyr, by Richard de Luci, Chief Justiciar of England, perhaps as penance for his involvement in the murder of Thomas Becket. It sits on rising land above what was originally marshland leading down to the river. Indeed, it was the abbey's responsibility for draining this marsh and maintaining the river embankments that caused it to have financial problems. As a result, it was never a large community.

It was closed by Cardinal Wolsey in 1525, one of the first monasteries to be dissolved after the Dissolution of the Monasteries in 1524. The monastic buildings were pulled down, except for the abbot's lodging, and the area became farmland, with the abbot's house forming part of a farmhouse. The monastery's original outline has now been restored to give a good idea of its size and atmosphere: the whole outline is visible and sections of walls and doorways have been rebuilt or restored. Few of the walls rise more than a few feet, but there are larger sections of arched stone doorways.

The physical situation of the abbey is intriguing, with ancient woodland alongside an 800-year-old Norman ruin, overlooking the bleak modern high rises of the Thamesmead development (where parts of Stanley Kubrick's iconic film, *A Clockwork Orange*, were shot). The contrasts are fascinating, and highlight London's age and constant development and change – some good, some bad.

More information about the site, and archaeological finds from excavations here, can be found by visiting The Greenwich Heritage Centre, Artillery Square, Royal Arsenal, Woolwich SE18 4DX (royalgreenwich.gov.uk/heritagecentre). The museums in nearby Erith and Plumstead also contain finds from the site.

CHISLEHURST CAVES

Chislehurst Caves are comprised of some 25mi of tunnels, 100ft below the upmarket, leafy suburb of Chislehurst (the name derives from the Saxon for a wood sitting on gravel). They aren't actually caves, but man-made mines, dug by hand to extract flint and chalk. Exact dating is impossible, but some experts believe that they originated in the Neolithic (New Stone Age) around 8,000 years ago, when flint was vital for making weapons and tools. Later, chalk was used for lime and as fertiliser and in cement.

Certain features in the caves are thought by some – including the more fanciful tour guides – to be Roman workings or Druid altars, but this is at best speculation. The caves' first recorded reference is from around 1250AD and they were mined until the 1830s, subsequently becoming a tourist attraction and then an ammunition dump for the Royal Arsenal at Woolwich in the First World War.

The '30s saw them used for mushroom cultivation, while in the Second World War they became an air raid shelter, effectively a sort of underground town of around 15,000 people, with electric light, a chapel and a hospital; only one baby was recorded as being born in the caves, appropriately named Rose Cavena Wakeman.

The '60s saw yet another incarnation for Chislehurst Caves, this time as a music venue, hosting the likes of such luminaries as (Bromley-born local boy) David Bowie, Jimi Hendrix, Pink Floyd, The Rolling Stones and Status Quo, while 1974 saw them host a lavish party to celebrate the launch of Led Zeppelin's Swan Song record company. In 2008, the charmingly-named heavy metal band Cradle of Filth made a music video here (as have several other bands), and the caves have also featured as sets in several television programmes, including 1973 episodes of *Dr Who* and, more recently, *Merlin*.

Two warnings about the caves: it's cool, underground – a constant 10ºC/50ºF – and the tours last awround 45 minutes, so dress appropriately, especially if you're visiting in summer. And they're supposed to be haunted, with a number of guides and visitors reporting that they've seen and heard strange things. Last, and perhaps least, there's a gift shop and café.

Touring the Lake District

ISBN: 978-1-913171-22-3, 128 pages, softback, £9.99, Jim Watson

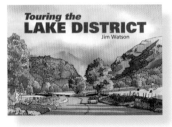

Touring the Lake District is a unique illustrated guide to exploring this beautiful area by car. Eight carefully planned tours take in the popular tourist centres plus a wealth of hidden gems that many consider to be the 'Real Lakeland'. The tours visit most of the famous lakes, negotiate empty country lanes, cross open moorland and test your driving skills on mountain passes. With picturesque villages, award-winning restaurants, gastro pubs and rustic coffee shops to enjoy along the way, this book will provide you with a comprehensive portrait of this varied and magnificent region.

Touring the Cotswolds

ISBN: 978-1-909282-91-9, 128 pages, softback, £9.99, Jim Watson

Touring the Cotswolds is a unique guide to exploring the best of the glorious Cotswolds by car through eight carefully planned tours, taking in the heavyweight tourist centres plus a wealth of hidden gems (the 'Real Cotswolds'). You'll negotiate a maze of country lanes, high hills with panoramic views, lush woodlands and beautiful valleys, plus an abundance of picturesque villages, providing a comprehensive portrait of this varied and delightful area.

INDEX

London's Architectural Walks, 2nd ed.

ISBN: 978-1-913171-01-8, 128 pages, softback, £9.99, Jim Watson

London's Architectural Walks is a unique guide to the most celebrated landmark buildings in one of the world's major cities. In thirteen easy walks, it takes you on a fascinating journey through London's diverse architectural heritage, with historical background and clear maps. The author's line and watercolour illustrations of all the city's significant buildings, make *London's Architectural Walks* an essential companion for anyone interested in the architecture that has shaped this great metropolis – and it's a great souvenir!

London's Secret Walks, 3rd ed.

ISBN: 978-1-909282-99-5, 320 pages, softback, £10.99, Graeme Chesters

London is a great city for walking – whether for pleasure, exercise or simply to get from A to B. Despite the city's extensive public transport system, walking is often the quickest and most enjoyable way to get around – at least in the centre – and it's also free and healthy! Many attractions are off the beaten track, away from the major thoroughfares and public transport hubs, which favours walking as the best way to explore them, as does the fact that London is a visually interesting city with a wealth of stimulating sights in every 'nook and cranny'.

London's Waterside Walks

ISBN: 978-1-909282-96-4, 192 pages, softback, £9.99, David Hampshire

Most people are familiar with London's River Thames, but the city has much more to offer when it comes to waterways, including a wealth of canals, minor rivers (most are tributaries of the Thames), former docklands, lakes and reservoirs. *London's Waterside Walks* takes you on 21 walks along many of the city's lesser-known, hidden waterways, including the Rivers Brent, Lea and Wandle, and the Grand Union and Regent's Canals.

London Escapes

ISBN: 978-1-913171-00-1, 192 pages, softback, £9.99, David Hampshire

London offers a wealth of attractions, but sometimes you just want to escape the city's constant hustle and bustle and visit somewhere with a gentler, slower pace of life. *London Escapes* offers over 70 days out less than two hours from the city, from historical towns and lovely villages to magnificent stately homes and

beautiful gardens; nostalgic seaside resorts and superb beaches to spectacular parks and nature reserves.

Great British Weekend Escapes

ISBN: 978-1-913171-21-6, 224 pages, softback, £10.99, David Hampshire

When you want to escape the daily grind for a few days, Britain offers a wealth of choices for memorable breaks, from captivating historic cities and charming towns to stunning countryside and beautiful coastline. Whether you're looking to discover a new city, indulge in a cultural or foodie weekend, enjoy a ramble in the countryside or an exhilerating coastal trip, you'll find them all in *Great British Weekend Escapes*' 70 enticing getaways.

From the bustling tourist hotspots of London and Liverpool to Edinburgh and Manchester; the historic university cities of Cambridge and Oxford; awe-inspiring cathedral cities such as Durham and Ely, Lincoln and Winchester; and captivating small towns like Rye, Southwold and Whitby. Nature lovers can escape to the spectacular Peak District, picturesque Cotswolds, charming New Forest, glorious Lake District, rugged Snowdonia and more.

see citybooks.co